T0246739

READING
ARENDT IN THE
WAITING ROOM

A Philosophy Primer for an Anxious Age

by
JONATHAN FOILES

Belt Publishing

Copyright 2024, Jonathan Foiles

First Edition, 2024
ISBN: 978-1-953368-83-6

Belt Publishing
6101 Penn Avenue, Suite 201, Pittsburgh PA 15206
www.beltpublishing.com

Cover design by David Wilson

And Polo said: "The inferno of the living is not something that will be; if there is one, it is what is already here, the inferno where we live every day, that we form by being together. There are two ways to escape suffering it. The first is easy for many: accept the inferno and become such a part of it that you can no longer see it. The second is risky and demands constant vigilance and apprehension: seek and learn to recognize who and what, in the midst of the inferno, are not inferno, then make them endure, give them space."

—Italo Calvino, *Invisible Cities*

There's no single answer that will solve all of our future problems. There's no magic bullet. Instead there are thousands of answers—at least. You can be one of them if you choose to be.

—Octavia Butler,
"A Few Rules for Predicting the Future"

For Esther

CONTENTS

CHAPTER 1
IT'S THE END OF THE WORLD
AS WE KNOW IT

This is a book about anxiety: mine, yours, and ours.

There are moments that strike like lightning to split the timeline of your life into a stark before and after. I will always remember—as if it were a first kiss or a car accident—when my anxiety began. I grew up in the 1990s within the contours of American evangelicalism, and for the first seven years of my life, my family attended a church of the fundamentalist Pentecostal variety. If asked back then, I would have said that being religious involved adherence to a series of prohibitions: don't use bad language, don't be disrespectful, don't watch television or movies, don't listen to rock music, don't cut your hair if you're a woman, or wear makeup. (There were more rules for the women, as there so often are.)

I quickly learned all these rules, which seemed so sacrosanct and unwavering to me, were not universal, however. There were things my family affirmed we wouldn't do in public, though we continued to do them privately. There was a second set of prohibitions my family abided by: Don't mention that we have a television, don't tell anyone you saw a movie for your sixth birthday, don't say that your mother still gets her hair cut. I don't fault my parents for this. Like many others, they were trying to create a space where they could live their lives within the tight strictures of their surrounding environment. And they were not alone. Even the pastor at our church had a television for "monitoring current events." And so we gathered together each Sunday morning, simultaneously proclaiming that a set of rules was the only thing keeping us from eternal damnation while also knowing that none of us were following them completely.

As a result, what I was told to do and what I actually did were never aligned—the perfect breeding ground for anxiety.

The God that haunted us was my first fear. At my church, there was no separate meeting for children during the adult services, so three times a week (Sunday morning, Sunday evening, and Wednesday evening), I would try to occupy myself as much as possible with my books, a few toys, and a well-timed snack as my parents listened closely and thought about how to modify their lives to be more in line with what we said we believed. I remember the feel of the hard wooden pews, sliding down to the floor, and looking between a forest of adult legs to spy glimpses of my friends with their own families. I was mostly free to do whatever I wanted during the services. Most of the time, whatever the pastor said went unnoticed by me; I might pick up on the feel of a particularly fiery passage from a sermon, but the words themselves washed over me. That is, until one Sunday evening, when the pastor warmed up a riff on hell and damnation that caught my attention as it never had before.

As he described it that night, hell was a place of never-ending fire and torment, the guaranteed destination for anyone who failed to follow Jesus. A great rapture was coming, he said. It was coming closer by the day, and it would offer escape to anyone who believed and death and destruction to anyone who was left behind. That day, as I sat perched in the pew next to my parents, their fear of divine judgment began to pulse through my own bloodstream. The pastor's exact words I have lost to time; the feeling I have not. And the links between the rules we said we lived by, our actual behavior, and the fear of what lay on the other side of our disobedience snapped together within my mind.

There was an easy solution to this anxiety, of course: "asking Jesus into your heart." The evangelical sermons I heard growing up all followed the same structure: the pastor would read a particular Bible passage, unspool what it meant for us, and then end with a bit of practical application, an answer to the "so what?" that marked everything that had come before. In the churches in which I grew up, this final "so what?" moment often centered around an altar call, an offer to leave behind your life of sin and become born again. That night, when the sermon reached this point, I was tempted to go to the front of the church to receive the call, but I ultimately resisted; a deeply shy child, I couldn't stand being the center of attention in our small congregation of fifty or so people. I also felt that coming out as a sinner would embarrass me beyond what I could stomach. I knew I had to do something, though, so I resolved to address the issue as soon as we returned home. In the back seat of my parents' Ford sedan, I contemplated the possibility of a car crash or the rapture occurring, leaving my young soul damned for eternity. My parents in the front and my grandmother next to me were already saved, I figured, and my younger sister would probably squeak through if anything happened because she was too young to be accountable for her own soul. But if there was such a test, I knew that, given the newfound knowledge that night's sermon had stirred within me, I would fail it. The drive home lasted only about fifteen minutes, but it felt much longer. As soon as we arrived, I stood in our garage next to our still-warm vehicle and said the first of many so-called "sinner's prayers." My parents told me how proud they were of me, and I basked in their adulation, freed from my fear.

My anxiety went away for a moment that night, but it was skilled at finding new permutations over time. What if my prayer that night hadn't taken? I wondered. As I got older, I learned that others in my orbit could trace their salvation to a particular date—a second birthday of sorts—but I could only remember mine had happened at some point when I was in kindergarten or first grade. "Are you *sure* you prayed the prayer then?" Sunday school teachers asked me. What if my sins became too grievous? What if I just finally wore God out until he was done with me? Nearly every week at church, I heard anew about the terrible burden of our sins, both individual and collective, and the ways in which our society—with its acceptance of abortion, gay people, and general licentiousness—continued to merit God's wrath. Against such a tide of evil, and with the threat of eternal damnation lying so close at hand, praying a few words once seemed woefully insufficient. I began to think I would never measure up and thus never find peace.

□ □ □ □ ■ □ □ □ □

Though you may have been spared the particulars of evangelical fear and judgment I went through, it's likely you've experienced similar feelings at some point in your life. Nearly all societies and cultures have found a way of describing this fear of impending doom. In the contemporary United States, we've gathered these sensations under the catchall heading of "anxiety." Anxiety disorders are the most prevalent mental disorders in our era, impacting nearly a third of people over the course of their life. In any given year, over 19 percent of the adult population in the United States meets the criteria for such a diagnosis. For adolescents, the number is even higher; nearly a third of teenagers in any given year experience the symptoms of an anxiety disorder. This figure rose by twenty percent between 2007 and 2012, and the well-documented impact of the COVID pandemic on adolescent mental health virtually guarantees another regrettable rise when social scientists collect and analyze further data in the future. Every age seems to have its own neurosis. Anxiety is ours.

I am a therapist, but I am also a human being. My anxiety and my early experiences within evangelicalism remain forever intertwined, and those experiences have been a far greater teacher than any textbook, internship, or peer-reviewed study. My anxiety has deeply shaped my life, and in many ways, the desire to help others who have experienced something similar has led me to this line of work.

Anxiety permeates our culture, but when I describe my own anxious experiences in the Pentecostal church, you may be likely to draw upon moments in your own life. As a concept, "anxiety" has become so widespread and ambiguous that it runs the risk of meaninglessness if we don't clarify what it actually entails. Throughout my time in therapy on both sides of the couch, I have come to hear (and often offer) the following explanation when it comes to anxiety: Our internal alarm system is a part of our preconscious brain that is meant to protect us from harm. It works really well to prepare a person for immediate danger, such as a careening car or a wild animal frothing at the mouth, but sometimes, it gets a little too good at its job.

I have a smoke detector next to my kitchen that is triggered if the stove becomes too hot or a searing steak lets off too much smoke. Anxiety can work like this too, sending off a loud warning of danger when the actual threat is minimal. My overly sensitive fire alarm makes the same amount of noise whether or not my house is actually in danger of burning down. Similarly, sometimes anxiety sets off its alarm bells for things that don't possess the same level of threat as a predator: spiders, airplanes, heights, confined spaces. At other times, the level of fear you feel isn't proportional to the actual event. Think about speaking in public. You may dread it and may even say something embarrassing, but the fear you experience about it far outweighs the possible impact of any mistake you might make. And then there are times when anxiety seems to lack any particular trigger, when fear suddenly clenches your chest for no discernible reason at all.

Over the years, psychology has come up with a variety of techniques to deal with this internal alarm system. If you find yourself anxious, for example, when you have to board an airplane, many therapists would suggest you ask yourself, "What's the worst that could happen?" Is it really likely the plane will crash? Airplane accidents are rare, and flying is statistically much safer than driving, even if it doesn't feel like it. In cases like these, empirical evidence is the balm. Alternatively, you could also work on acclimating yourself to flying, starting out by sitting with the thought of taking a flight, then watching airplane videos on YouTube, then perhaps driving by the airport until you learn to cope with the anxious thoughts and develop a greater sense of efficacy in the face of them. Or, if such triggers aren't easily available to you, you can do things that reduce your overall anxiety level: exercise, eat right, get enough sleep, practice mindfulness.

Nothing in this approach to anxiety is wrong per se; if you were my patient and were seeking to address such a concrete fear, I would suggest you try many of these suggestions, although as a psychoanalytic therapist, I would also be interested in probing where your fear comes from and how it helps structure your internal sense of self. However, all these approaches assume there is no *true* threat beyond what we all face in our everyday lives. The focus of the treatment is on you and changing how you think and/or behave so that it is more in line with what is real. We can label this *personal* anxiety—anxiety that has to do with an individual and their perception of the world, which can be altered through tweaking their threat-assessment tools.

This anxiety can indeed lead a person to seek therapy and other forms of help, but it makes up less of my

work than you might think. More often, the source of
the anxieties I see in my daily practice are less well-de-
fined and thus not so amenable to a simple course of
exposure therapy.

So what happens if your anxiety isn't solely a matter
of distorted thoughts you've accrued that have no basis in
the real world? What if your fear isn't about something
concrete like airplanes or spiders but is instead about
something more uncontrollable, maybe even cataclysmic?
While I no longer believe in much of what I was raised
to fear, when I looked around as a child and adolescent,
I saw not that my beliefs were misplaced but that they
were all too real. I read the then bestselling *Left Behind*
books by Tim LaHaye and Jerry B. Jenkins, which
described how Christ would redeem a select group of
true believers, leaving most of the earth's population
to live in a world racked with evil and abandoned by
God. I heard sermon after sermon about the evilness
of the "secular" world and the ever-present temptation
toward sin. I listened to music that wrapped up such
theology in the sounds of contemporary pop tunes. But
no amount of behavioral modification or checking my
catastrophizing would have helped because everything
around me was asserting that my fears were indeed
real—good, even. The only way to confront the anxiety
I was feeling was to change the entire frame. To really
deal with my crippling fear, I had to alter my way of
thinking about the world.

What I was experiencing wasn't a faulty fire alarm going off in my head but rather my own internal sense that what I was hearing and being taught was not life-giving and affirming but something else entirely. If I had tried applying conventional therapeutic tools to my thinking, they would only have reinforced my misery and made me live more compliantly within it. This has too often happened throughout the history of psychology when, for instance, queer individuals are forced to live inside identities that don't fit, or when people of color are told their protests against a deeply unjust society are not a rational response to injustice but rather a sign of disordered thinking.

I see similar questions of existence and anxiety about meaning-making within my own practice. There was the patient in his late twenties who entered a prestigious PhD program with dreams of spending days in academic debate with like-minded fellows but was instead faced with a toxic, backbiting department and little guarantee of a future job on the other side of eight years of hard work. There was another patient who finally decided to turn around and face the nagging question of their gender identity that never really went away despite their efforts to ignore it. Another person I worked with returned to evangelical Christianity after a period away from it and thought of the experience as returning to the fold after flirting with a life of sin, though she has begun to think that such a frame is not only unhelpful but an echo of the harsh critiques she experienced from her parents throughout her childhood and adolescence. None of these patients fits the standard account of the etiology and treatment of anxiety. Each of them has to confront a far bigger, more existential question than a simple phobia of heights, flying, or speaking in front of an audience. Should I give up on the career I've dreamed of since childhood? Should I explore how I express my gender or the words I use to describe my identity? Should I continue to embrace the evangelical narrative of fall, sin, and redemption even if I don't feel that fallen? Questions like these can be clear causes of anxiety, but they require more than just a reassessment of the facts—they entail a wholesale reconsideration of the entire shape of one's life.

Therapy can be a helpful guide for patients in these situations too, though it requires them to do considerable work. I can and do help people explore such impasses, but I cannot conclusively answer the deep questions they're grappling with. That isn't really my job, and I wouldn't be helping them if I opined on their future in academia or suggested what their gender identity should be. In these cases, the search is a part of the journey, but it is ultimately *their* journey. But the anxiety they're facing is *existential,* related not just to matters of perception but to concerns about the fundamental ways they fit within the world.

In both my own work and daily life, I get a sense of what triggers are causing anxiety to pulse within each of us. Sometimes it's straightforward stuff like airplanes or spiders, but many other times it's these bigger, more existential issues. And the COVID-19 pandemic upended all of that in a profound way that still has me teasing out the implications for my work and the business of therapy itself.

The early days of lockdown were filled with anxiety for all of us. In March of 2020, I emailed clients an elaborate list of precautions I would be taking in my office and then had to follow it up a few days later with the news that I was closing in-person appointments entirely. My group practice bought a business license for Zoom so we could start practicing teletherapy. I claimed a corner in my bedroom as my makeshift office. Many of my patients who were connected to the nearby university scattered to their various homes, and I had to sift through the ever-changing rules governing telehealth across state lines to identify which states were being flexible and which ones wouldn't allow me to see my patients.

Those sorts of upheavals would be enough to challenge anyone, but the spread of a mysterious and deadly disease poured gasoline upon an already raging fire. First, there was the uncertainty of how the virus was spreading, then the realization that there was no real way to treat it and no vaccine to prevent it. Stores ran out of disinfectants, food, toilet paper. We were told masks weren't effective, then that we should all wear cloth masks, then later that cloth masks actually weren't sufficient and we should use N95 masks instead. I opened my office for masked in-person sessions, then had to close it a few months later when another wave hit.

Through all of this, therapists like me were not neutral parties standing apart from the masses. I faced the same fears as my patients when it felt like the world as we knew it was collapsing. This was something bigger than a nagging alarm bell or even a deep existential crisis; the specter of mass death and catastrophic human suffering loomed over us all.

There was nothing I learned in graduate school or my practice that prepared me for such a moment. This was *apocalyptic* anxiety, not anxiety bound by one's own perceptions or attempts to find a place in the world but rather a threat that seemed to undermine our collective societal existence. It awakened within me the long-dormant fear that the world was literally ending in front of my eyes, and even if I no longer feared some deity was the author of such destruction, the feeling seemed eerily similar to what I had experienced when anxiety first took root within me in that Pentecostal church.

The pandemic isn't the only catastrophe that has impinged upon our collective well-being in the recent past, and it's not the only example of the kind of apocalyptic anxiety that increasingly seems to permeate our collective existence. These concerns are not reducible to phobias, and they extend beyond the individual and appear to threaten society as a whole. If the climate is undergoing a rapid shift, even important existential questions—like what to do for one's career—seem to pale in significance. Other, similar questions continue to haunt us and seem to threaten the very basis for our shared life together. Will the United States remain a democracy? Will nine people elected to lifetime positions on the Supreme Court, most of them by presidents who lost the popular vote, gradually erode the rights of everyone who is not a straight white male? Can people under forty live any sort of meaningful life amidst the rubble of late capitalism, with six-figure student loan debt, skyrocketing housing costs, and stagnant wages for the jobs and industries that will remain after a handful of billionaires finally own everything? How are we supposed to live when it feels like the end of the world as we know it?

Gradual exposure to these apocalyptic fears will not make them go away, will not dissolve their looming menace. There is also no way to change the frame with these questions, to simply consider them from another angle. They threaten the very roots of our existence. They are related to our individual existence, of course, but they have much deeper ramifications than considerations about one's own future or identity. After all, it does not matter what career one follows or the identity one explores if there is no world left in which to act. It is, of course, possible to suffer from all three types of anxiety I have outlined here at the same time; one can have an irrational fear of germs, existential questions about what to do for one's career, and a feeling of apocalyptic terror that climate change will render the earth inhospitable. Anxiety doesn't take turns, where germaphobia taps out to let larger fears take over for a while. Therapy gives us ample tools to deal with the fears that arise in the course of everyday life. It can also be invaluable when attempting to unspool the more foundational stuff of one's life: whom one should date or marry, what career one should pursue, what gender identity or sexuality fits with one's inner sense of self. And while I don't find therapy to be toothless in the face of impending apocalypse, I do often find myself needing a different vocabulary than the merely personal when working through such issues with my patients, one that hearkens back to my own attempts to quiet the fears that raged in my head after being ignited by the possibility of hellfire.

This effort to merge the personal approach of psychotherapy with a vocabulary that can adequately address larger societal concerns has roots in the work of Sigmund Freud and his followers. Freud believed a broad background in the humanities was the best preparation for becoming a therapist, and he sought to apply psychoanalytic principles to the culture at large in his writings and to live out their liberatory ethics through the founding of free clinics that were open to all, regardless of their ability to pay. I view this book as being an extension of that oft-neglected approach.

Aside from psychoanalysis, contemporary psychotherapy often comes up against a wall when attempting to address such apocalyptic concerns. There is no prayer or mindfulness exercise that can lower the earth's temperature. We should be gravely concerned about our climate future, and any method or intervention that focuses solely upon the subjective experience of individuals on a burning planet blinds us to the structural choices that have led us to this point and any agency we might have to make a different future for ourselves. It's no surprise that the wellness-industrial complex has exploded just as these questions have begun to penetrate many people's consciousness. ExxonMobil would much rather have us attend a sponsored yoga class or download a mindfulness app than begin to ask too many questions that could lead us to structural considerations about the impacts of fossil fuels. Wellness itself isn't antithetical to political struggle, but like anything, it can become weaponized and render us complacent. What we need instead are tools to help us think bigger, to help us grapple with the deepest fears we all feel together.

This is where I think the history of philosophy can be particularly helpful and instructive. It offers ample resources for thinking through what constitutes a life well-lived, even when one's very existence seems threatened. At its best, philosophy gives us a framework to consider the meaning of our lives and choices and the freedom we have to make a difference within the contours of our experience. As a therapist in a university community, I find many of my patients drawn to philosophy and philosophical ways of thinking for similar reasons, but even if you don't live or practice in the shadow of a major university, philosophy can still prove to be startlingly useful.

I don't want to come across as an apostle for philosophy, and this is not a second conversion narrative, although I realize that type of language can be tempting: "I found evangelical Christianity insufficient, so I instead adopted philosophy as my guiding principle." Such an explanation is not only incorrect—although my relationship to faith has changed profoundly, I am now a pretty comfortable progressive Episcopalian—but it merely swaps air-tight conviction in one set of principles with a different set of propositional truths. What I can say, though, is that philosophy helped me with my anxiety, and I believe the attention it pays to the biggest questions that have haunted people for centuries, and that continue to vex us now, positions it to be uniquely helpful in sorting out how to face community-wide catastrophe at the end of history.

I felt drawn to philosophy before I ever considered making my living as a therapist. In high school, as I tried to untangle what a life of faith might look like absent the certainty my upbringing promised, I reached for the work of Søren Kierkegaard. In college, I read Martin Heidegger and thought about what I wanted my life to be like in the face of the certain death that awaits us all. Later, in graduate school, I found a way to think about life and ethics through the lens of Aristotle. My anxiety was a companion alongside each stage in my journey, and reading the work of these thinkers helped me. I think it can help you too, which is why I've written this book.

Philosophy has also helped me learn to love the world again. If the world is the place we leave behind before we get to the "good stuff" of eternal bliss in heaven—a belief I first heard as a six-year-old in church—it doesn't have to matter all that much. If most of the people surrounding you won't be there, you don't really have to care about them. Few are as selfish in practice as their theologies might suggest, but as I grew up, I didn't feel like an integral part of the world or the society around me—sometimes, I was even scared of them. I recognize the same dynamic, albeit in a different key, in many of the progressive circles in which I now locate myself. Recent history has given us plenty of reasons to regard each other with suspicion or even hostility, but to really work on leaving apocalyptic anxiety behind, we have to dare to hope that something can be different, that people are capable of radical, culture-wide change. If you don't find yourself able to believe that just yet, I understand. I hope the following pages will help change your mind.

I am, of course, a therapist, not a philosopher. And as we travel across the history of philosophy, I want to be clear that I'm not going to be guided by the robustness of the various arguments I present or their place within intellectual history. Instead, I'm interested in the actual, real-life difference those ideas might be able to make for that patient sitting in front of me who is feeling the crushing weight of despair as they think about the future. I do not claim to be the first therapist to do this. The existential approach to therapy, in particular, seeks to do roughly the same thing, adapting philosophical concepts concerning meaning-making and being, often from some of the same philosophers I consider here. But while it has a storied history, approaches like that are rarely implemented or taught today; they didn't factor at all into my own training, and they go against the wider grain of contemporary psychotherapy, which has increasingly become focused on the provision of tools and the reformatting of personal thoughts at the expense of such widescreen concerns. I also want to challenge this individualistic ethos that abandons any sense of community or collectivity. I find no small degree of comfort in realizing that the deep, apocalyptic anxieties I talk about here are nothing new. The particular conditions that give rise to them may change, but the fear that life as we know it might end is something our species knows well. Listening to the distant and not-so-distant past will give us not just a way to think about our own uncertainties in a new light but also hope, a new way to survive together.

Which brings me back to that apocalypse I used to fear so much. As a child, I was taught that the more apocalyptic passages in the Hebrew Bible and the New Testament form a sort of puzzle, a series of images and warnings for the faithful to decode in order to understand what awaits us in the future. The word "apocalypse," though, actually means something closer to "unveiling." The ancient prophets who wrote stories of beasts and plagues, of societal devastation, state violence, and political collapse, weren't thinking about the future at all; they were seeking to pull back the veil upon their own time to illuminate the hidden forces at work in events that, on their own, seemed futile, cruel, and insurmountable. To people who were looking for meaning when the world seemed totally meaningless, the apocalyptic texts rendered judgment upon the powerful and provided hope that all was not lost, and better days were ahead. Consider this little book my own attempt at such an apocalyptic unveiling.

My end goal here is not an altar call, but this journey across my autobiography, intertwined with a brief intellectual history and my own experiences as a therapist, has a similar goal in terms of application. Chances are you picked up this book in the quest for something to quell those 3 a.m. fears of impending doom, to enable you to move through a chaotic, unpredictable world with something approximating hope. My purpose in writing this is not just to get more people to read philosophy and consider the wider factors that can influence our mental health—even if they often go undiagnosed and underexplored. I also want to help you find a new way of thinking. We cannot just stop there, however; if we are to avoid some of the worst predictions for what our future might hold, we must act. We must work to put something into being rather than only talking about it. I hope you hear the call to action echoing through the following pages.

CHAPTER 2
TAKING A LEAP: SØREN KIERKEGAARD

I grew up in a small town without police. Towns like mine, with a population of five hundred or so people, don't have the resources to sustain their own department. The nearby town where my high school was located had a small police force, but their main responsibility seemed to involve sitting alongside the highway just outside the city limits to ticket speeding drivers as they passed through. If something happened that required a police response, the county sheriff would answer the call, usually within twenty minutes or so. Although I followed the rules way too closely to ever test this personally, the rumor around my high school was that a sheriff's deputy often drove through town at two reliable points in the middle of the night, so those who would be breaking curfew would know when it was most safe to do so. For the most part, this all worked; my town wasn't crime-free by any means, but it also wasn't an anarchic free-for-all.

Now I live in the Hyde Park neighborhood of Chicago, in close proximity to the University of Chicago, with a policing setup that is the polar opposite of my experience growing up. My neighborhood is regularly patrolled by three different security forces. The Chicago Police Department maintains a noticeable presence. There is also the University of Chicago Police Department and—a more recent feature, hired in the wake of concerns over rising crime—a private security force that patrols the neighborhood, flashing green lights atop their vehicles to announce their rounds. I'm close enough to campus that there are emergency call boxes located on several corners near my house, and as one drifts closer toward student housing when school is in session, there are often security guards stationed at every corner. Regardless of this saturation, crime still happens—occasionally shootings but far more often burglaries, acts of vandalism, and property crime. I do not feel unsafe in my neighborhood, a luxury that I try to keep in mind, but neither do I feel completely at ease.

I contrast the experiences of my youth and those of my adulthood to point out the often tenuous connection between police and public safety. As demands to reduce police budgets or to completely abolish some departments have grown over the past few years, many pundits and laypeople alike have demonstrated a lack of imagination in asking what we would do to keep ourselves safe in the absence of the swollen police presence that is a feature of every major American city. Most of the time, the answer to this is nothing—communities like the one in which I grew up, as well as many suburbs, have minimal interactions with or need for the police. There is a subtext to this question about public safety: "Who will keep us safe from *them*?" In a country with racial politics such as ours, the *them* is almost always someone who isn't white, and disproportionately, it is someone who is Black. Monochromatic villages and suburbs rarely navigate the friction of racial difference and thus do not get subjected to the same line of questioning that cities like Chicago do.

The police are unique amongst public figures in that they are the only agents we trust to exercise force when needed. While state-sanctioned bodies meant to secure the public good have existed since at least the earliest days of colonization, the modern institution known as the police originated as slave-catcher patrols meant to find and return escaped enslaved persons to servitude. Since their founding they have been utilized to discipline and punish Black people, but technological advances that now allow most of us to carry high-fidelity video cameras around in our pockets have given many of us a front-row view into this reality for the first time. Any list of names of Black people killed by police would surely end up being out of date in between the composition of this paragraph and its publication, and the news offers a steady stream of premature Black death at the hands of those who have sworn an oath to protect everyone. An increasing number of people recognize a deeply damaged dynamic here that needs to be fixed, yet we continue to lack imagination for how to deal with the problem. As

the private security force in my neighborhood demonstrates, when we're confronted with safety concerns, the
answer we reach for is almost always more funding for
more officers. Politicians of every stripe fear looking "soft
on crime" by reducing police budgets, and even those
progressive reformers who manage to get elected to office
often find themselves chafing against cascading levels
of bureaucracy invested in the status quo. It is enough
to make anyone feel hopeless. How are we to confront
the seemingly limitless power of the police to kill with
impunity and continue to get away with it?

The sparseness of my hometown meant that if we
wanted to do much of anything—buy groceries, shop,
see a movie—we had to drive at least twenty miles in
any direction. Most often, we went to Decatur, the
"Soy Capital of the World." Processing plants belched
great clouds of smoke into the air, forming a skyline as
recognizable as skyscrapers upon approach. When we
had more time on the weekends, we would occasionally
travel to Champaign-Urbana, home to the University
of Illinois's flagship campus. The academic environment there felt leagues different than that of industrial
Decatur. For my adolescent self, that mostly meant it
had bookstores.

The pseudo-suburban sprawl of Champaign's shop-
ping district contained a Borders and a Barnes & Noble
less than a mile from each other. Although I would end
up working at that Barnes & Noble when I was a college

student, I preferred going to Borders for reasons I could not express, though they were perfectly clear to me at the time. It was at that Borders, which, in the wake of the company's bankruptcy, was converted into a liquor store, that as a high school student I found my way to the philosophy section and picked up *The Living Thoughts of Kierkegaard*, an anthology of the philosopher's musings and aphorisms edited by W. H. Auden. I felt out of my depth exploring the shelves full of titles both fascinating and opaque, and I snatched my copy of the book and walked away before anyone could potentially identify me as an interloper.

I can't remember exactly when or where I first heard of Søren Kierkegaard; it feels as if he has always been a part of my thinking. His thoughts on a religious faith that involves an assumption of risk in the absence of definitive proof for the presence or absence of God flitted around the edges of some of the more conventional religious books I was reading at the time. The more I found out about him, the less he felt like an obvious progenitor of cheap inspirational literature, and the more I felt drawn to him.

Evangelicalism taught me that the Bible was inerrant, that each word of Scripture was fully inspired by God to form a perfect truth. I had no trouble believing that as a child, but as I grew older and did what my church encouraged me to do—read the Bible for myself—I realized it contained far more discordant notes than the dogma I had received could accommodate. I am not talking about a misplaced word here or a small inconsistency but big things, and sometimes even the *biggest* things—for instance, the narratives concerning the death of Jesus Christ, the event upon which the entire book hangs. Depending upon which Gospel you consult, Jesus seems to die convinced his mission was a failure; in agony but resigned; or perfectly at peace, whispering "it is finished" before breathing his last. The Gospels also differ on who was present at the crucifixion and what they said. If this book was supposed to be without error, it seemed the concept of "error" was rather slippery, to say the least. This was in the early days of the internet, and I consulted various websites and books that attempted to answer these tough questions, but the explanations I found always felt like evasions rather than sincere efforts to confront an authentic dilemma. From the little I knew about Kierkegaard, it seemed he had found a different way to approach the concept of belief other than complete assent to a series of propositions. And though I couldn't imagine what this might be at the time, I was intrigued.

Kierkegaard was born in Copenhagen in 1813, spent most of his life there, and died at the age of forty-two. His father had been born a serf but became a successful merchant before Kierkegaard's birth. Despite achieving outward success in business, his father felt deeply afflicted. Kierkegaard was born into a privileged family and pursued a relatively stable academic path but lost momentum over the course of his studies. A devout journal-keeper from the age of twenty-one until his death, he would write of pursuing all the pleasures of the flesh—parties, fine clothes, the theater—while also finding such pursuits rather hollow. He finally completed his degree in theology in 1840, and later that year, he became engaged to a woman named Regine Olsen. While outwardly it appeared he was settling down, inwardly, he remained tempest-tossed.

The following year, Kierkegaard broke off his engagement; Regine would be one of the major inspirations for his writing, even as his personal life charted a path away from her. His reasons for ending the engagement aren't entirely clear, but once he made the decision, he seemed to view it as a matter of fate. The best guess we have is from his journals, where he said he did it to spare her from his melancholy.

Instead of getting married, he wrote. In the following years, a torrent of works poured forth from him. Six works appeared in 1843, five in 1844, and two each in the subsequent three years. Many of them were published under a series of pseudonyms, a not-uncommon practice at the time to distance the author from the arguments they were making. When he wasn't writing, he could usually be found walking around Copenhagen.

When I first encountered Kierkegaard's work, I immediately felt a kinship with him, especially with the sadness that seemed to color his life and the way his pursuit of the truth seemed to separate him from everyone else in his community. I too felt I didn't belong where I grew up, yet it was hard for me to put my finger on exactly why that was. My friends at the time were the other members of my small class who took faith seriously, and while this gave us some common ground, none of them seemed to wrestle with the same doubts I did, nor did they share my interests in literature and indie rock. This often stoked the flames of my panic, making me fear I would never find a group of people who really understood me to my bones. But even if that wasn't going to happen, I figured, I could at least try to understand myself.

One of Kierkegaard's earliest books is *Fear and Trembling* (1843), in which he examines a particularly troubling Biblical narrative concerning Abraham, the patriarch and figurehead of the three aptly named Abrahamic faiths that trace their lineage to him: Judaism, Christianity, and Islam. He first appears in the twelfth chapter of the first book of the Hebrew Bible, where God commands Abraham—who at that point is called Abram—to leave behind everything he has known to migrate to a new land with the promise that he will become the forerunner of a great civilization. Abraham remains active but heirless for several chapters after that. In a moment of desperation, Abraham's wife Sarah suggests he try instead to conceive an heir with their

Egyptian slave, Hagar, but when this works and Hagar gives birth to a son named Ishmael, Sarah treats the enslaved woman and her child brutally with Abraham's approval, leaving the issue of lineage an open question. In Genesis 21, Sarah finally gives birth to their son, Isaac, but in the very next chapter, this future—which had already seemed so doubtful—becomes immediately threatened.

In the following chapter, God decides to test Abraham by commanding him to go and sacrifice Isaac as a burnt offering: "[God] said, 'Take your son, your only son Isaac, whom you love, and go to the land of Moriah and offer him there as a burnt offering on one of the mountains that I shall show you.'"[1] This undercuts everything we have read up to this point about Abraham and his promised future, but he follows the command without question: "So Abraham rose early in the morning, saddled his donkey, and took two of his young men with him and his son Isaac."[2] He locates the mountain and takes Isaac to the top. It is not until Isaac is bound on a pile of wood, Abraham standing over him with knife aloft, that God tells him to stop. Abraham has passed the test, proving to God that he fears him, so God blesses him and promises to make his descendants many since he proved faithful by offering to murder his child. It's a bleak tale, and it's one that resists easy interpretation. It's also one of the stories that used to make me question the God at the center of my family's faith, and worry that I could not continue to believe in him.

Rather than try to evade the question or chalk it up to God's unknowability, though, in *Fear and Trembling*, Kierkegaard confronts the challenge of the Abraham story head-on. I appreciated the strength of his resolve, which was so unlike the sermons I heard every week that sanded—or sometimes completely ignored—the rough edges of scripture.

In the first few pages of *Fear and Trembling*, Kierkegaard writes out several different ways to make sense of this narrative. It's a sort of midrash—a traditional Jewish form of Biblical criticism that "talks back" to the text—although he doesn't call it that. Perhaps, Kierkegaard suggests, Abraham told Isaac that it was not God who told him to kill his son but purely his own desire; by doing this, Abraham attempts to preserve Isaac's faith in God while destroying his faith in his own father. Or maybe, Kierkegaard writes, Abraham moves through the story as we've been told but can never again confront, much less worship, the God who commanded him to kill his son. In another potential reading, Abraham is reminded of Ishmael and filled with guilt and remorse at his actions and his willingness to sacrifice Isaac. He ascends the mountain alone and begs God for forgiveness. In the final explication, Isaac sees his father's revulsion at what God has commanded him to do and loses his faith in such a deity. But after considering these possibilities, Kierkegaard rejects any account of the binding of Isaac that would render the story intelligible within our given frame of reference. The power of the narrative lies in the fact that it isn't reducible to any of these other renderings he has considered, or indeed to any objective sense of logic at all.

Having held the story to the light and considered it from all angles, Kierkegaard compares the narrative to other similar stories we have inherited, looking for the kernel of the ethical within them. On the face of it, the story of Abraham is familiar, albeit sad: parents murdering their children is nothing new. What is new in this story, though, is the fact that Abraham is the hero, not the villain. This is not meant to be a depressing story of filicide but an example of the depths of one person's religious faith. Is Abraham a tragic hero? No, Kierkegaard says, for "the tragic hero stays within the ethical."[3] The tragic hero is tragic because of their refusal to step outside the norms and laws of their society to act in their own interest. After Lucius Junius Brutus helped establish the Roman Republic by overthrowing the final king of Rome, Lucius Tarquinius Superbus, two of his sons worked to restore the monarchy and were sentenced to death by Brutus, who then witnessed their execution. Brutus has been portrayed as a paragon of republican virtue and a tragic hero for centuries since: he suspends familial prejudices and subjective desires to secure the common good. Abraham, though, does no such thing. Brutus is tragic because he oversees the execution of his sons, but he's a hero because he does so to prevent further bloodshed and establish the Roman Republic. There is no such higher principle at work in the story of Abraham other than God telling him to follow a command. We are, in the end, asked to take Abraham's word for it. Narratives like that of Brutus can be used to prop up the status quo; when I think of the quiet fortitude they display, I am reminded of the media narratives that highlight how the "good cop" helped take care of the child in need or stood cool in the face of protesters. Stories like that of Abraham, however, resist integration into any preexisting schema; they require us to confront the horizon of possibility in an act of radical imagination.

Kierkegaard rejects the idea that there is a universal logic at work in the willingness of Abraham to sacrifice his son. "He resigned everything infinitely," he writes, "and then took everything back on the strength of the absurd."[4] There remains a fundamental unknowability at the heart of the story. Abraham's duty to God suspends all rationality in what Kierkegaard calls the "teleological suspension of the ethical." It is ultimately Abraham's faith and his duty to God above all else, even when the way forward seems entirely unclear, that makes him a "knight of faith." Abraham doesn't speak in the narrative, other than to assure Isaac that God will provide a sacrifice, because he does not have the language to explain it. In the end, he stands alone before his God. The story does not have to make sense in any straightforwardly rational sense; it is not reducible to an easy moral one can grasp in three points. Kierkegaard does not strip the Biblical narrative of its complexity nor try to make it fit within a neat story arc, and while this sort of ambiguity can be a breeding ground for anxiety, my adolescent brain found it strangely hopeful.

If Kierkegaard is correct, this says something profound about the practice of ethics. Ethics is no longer about the adherence to universal norms or rules if such norms or rules can be subverted; living a proper life is solely about how one comports oneself in relation to God. Other philosophers working before Kierkegaard noticed the subversive kernel in the story of Abraham as well. Immanuel Kant, for example, based his ethical project upon the notion of the categorical imperative, the idea that the right way to act in any given situation is in such a way that it could be made a universal law. If I would like to live in a world where people stopped on the street to help a person in need, that is how I should act when confronted with such a situation. Kant realized the challenge posed by the story of Abraham and suggested it was not—that it could not be—God who was speaking to him: "Abraham should have replied to this supposedly divine voice: 'That I ought not to kill my good son is quite certain. But that you, this apparition, are God—of that I am not certain, and never can be, not even [if] this voice rings down to me from (visible) heaven."[5]

When I first encountered Kierkegaard in high school, I had no idea I was wading into the waters of a core debate concerning the ethical life. What drew me to him was the way he dismantled the certainty I saw all around me: certainty that my family and I were going to heaven while most other people weren't, certainty that every word of the Bible was inspired, infallible truth, certainty that we voted for the right politicians and supported the right policies to remake the surrounding society into the kingdom of God as envisioned by the religious right. I felt like I lacked this certainty gene as far back as I can remember. I agonized over not being public enough with my faith. I worried the world would end and I would find myself on the wrong side of the line between heaven and hell.

Like the narrator of *Fear and Trembling*, I can't claim to look at Abraham and understand him. I couldn't when I first read the story, and his actions have grown even more inscrutable to me—dangerous, even—now that I have children of my own. Most of the time, I would much rather live in the world envisioned by Kant, where we rigorously fact-check every utterance we believe we've received from on high to determine whether or not it is ethical, a world where we can trust the police and those who wield authority have our best interests in mind. And yet.

I find myself returning to *Fear and Trembling* every few years since I first read those excerpts in high school. I haven't considered rereading Kant after completing my undergraduate degree. Encountering Kierkegaard unlocked something within me. I came to think the certainty I had grown up trying so desperately to believe in, and often failing, got something crucial wrong. Faith isn't about certainty; the contradiction is evident in the mere definition of those terms. To believe in something as big as God and the contention that God has intervened in the stuff of human history takes an extraordinary amount of risk, a willingness to be quite wrong. Over time, I loosened my grip on trying to stuff the Bible into a symphony and instead worked to listen to its individual parts.

Even if most of us don't agonize over the narrative of Abraham—or think of it at all—there's something more that makes *Fear and Trembling* resonate with our current times. Kant's categorical imperative assumes a sort of universal beneficence on the part of humankind: I can be confident in acting in a way I would like universalized because I know that everyone else is also trying hard to be a good person and build a better world for all of us. I don't know about you, but I lack that basic belief. I don't think oil industry executives or fascists or bigots have such goodwill in mind when they seek to remake our society in their own image; there's something far more elemental and selfish in their attempts to secure the best for themselves and damn everyone else to what's left. This doesn't mean we need to abandon all considerations of the good, but it does suggest we need to be far more clear-eyed about the actions and intentions of those around us when considering the future of the world and our place within it.

Even if this weren't true, the categorical imperative can only operate within the confines of the given combination of one's life experiences to date and the lessons one has absorbed from the surrounding culture. Consider the following. There was a stretch of time when the front door to our apartment building did not lock. It was not obvious that it was open, and the interior door leading to the hallway remained locked, but if someone checked, they could have entered our vestibule. One morning, as I was taking the dog out, I discovered an unhoused person sleeping in front of the mailboxes. Every message I received growing up would have encouraged me to see that person as a threat in some way, to invoke the help of the police in having a trespasser removed from the premises. If that was the background knowledge I brought to such an encounter, then I would assume following that script was the right—the ethical—thing to do and would hope that my fellow residents would act similarly if they encountered the situation first. I do not possess any special virtue in dealing with houseless people, but I have worked in case management for people experiencing homelessness and mental illness. I've tried to educate myself a bit on what causes homelessness, and I believe police do nothing to help such situations and only increase the possibility that the person who is already suffering will be injured or murdered. Because of these experiences, when I approached this situation in my own apartment building, I had a different script I could draw from. My categorical imperative is thus different, not because I am a fundamentally better person than those who would operate within a carceral logic but because both knowledge and experience have altered my frame of reference.

When trying to describe the way the mind was structured, Sigmund Freud made a few different attempts before he settled upon the formula most of us know: id, ego, and superego. The translation from German into "English" (really, Latin) stiffened the language he used; a more helpful translation would be the it, the I, and the above-I. The it contains the elemental drives that remind us of our past as animals, the I contains most of what we think of as containing "ourselves," and the above-I gathers the lessons we learn first from our parents and caregivers and later from society at large about how to govern our behavior and best get along with others. Our superego, our above-I, often causes us to suffer mentally: if we grow up in a family that prioritizes productivity and success above all else, we may feel guilty about taking time to rest and recharge; if we grow up in an evangelical purity culture that teaches abstinence and expects people to switch on their sexuality only after they are married, we may always associate sex with shame. It can help to confront whether or not these scripts we have developed are true—it's important in situations like those I named above to reconsider one's relationship to work or sexuality—but if you've ever tried to defeat such encroaching and inherited negativity within yourself, you've probably noticed it's rather impervious to logic. Along with considering such questions of rationality, I encourage my patients to ask themselves whether or not such beliefs are working for them. When you're feeling guilty in the evening because you really want to stop working but worry about the ramifications, it's not always helpful to re-interrogate the assumptions behind such an impulse and instead just ask yourself, "Is this helpful for me right now?" I'm feeling exhausted, burned out, and hungry; would it be better to push through, or should I listen to what my body is trying to tell me? To make it to such a place, though, requires both a sense that something is wrong and a hope that a better way of living is possible. This can be a difficult position to reach, but at times, like Abraham, all of us are capable of listening to voices outside ourselves that may lead us in directions we don't expect with the promise of something radically different at the end of the journey.

I should note that for Kierkegaard, this remains a solitary endeavor. While we know from his letters and papers that he had close friends and a fulfilling social life, the person working through the issues Kierkegaard explores is always a singularity. As we will see in due time, this inability to imagine the possibility of communal action is not limited to his thought. It is indeed an issue throughout philosophy that the acting individual is almost always seen as obeying the dictates of their own conscience, whether that be Kierkegaard's knight of faith, Kant's person trying to sort out the categorical imperative in a given situation, or Descartes's lonely, disembodied mind searching for something to ground its existence. This tension between the individual and their society finds its fullest expression within Kierkegaard's attack upon state-sponsored religion.

Fear and Trembling marked a shift in Kierkegaard's thought away from the aesthetic and ethical consider-ations of his first major work, *Either/Or* (1843), toward an examination of how to live authentically as a Christian in his time. Without abandoning philosophical consid-erations entirely, in the years following, he published works on freedom, anxiety, and the introduction of sin into the human race (*The Concept of Anxiety*, 1844); despair and the life of faith (*The Sickness Unto Death*, 1849); and a series of "uplifting discourses" that more closely resemble sermons or devotional essays than phil-osophical arguments. A simmering tension throughout his writings on religion that boiled over near the end of his life was the role of the official state church, the

Church of Denmark, in the life of faith of the individual. His polemics help us think through how to best address and confront oppressive structures, such as the police, in our own time.

Kierkegaard saw everything affiliated with state-sponsored religion, which he referred to as "Christendom," as hindering rather than facilitating the individual's encounter with God; at the height of his conflicts with the institutional church, he wrote in his journals, "Christendom is Satan's invention."[6] He began to develop his critique in the aforementioned *The Sickness Unto Death*. In the preface of that book, he claims that most of us, the church included, fail to treat faith with the seriousness it deserves: "Everything essentially Christian must have in its presentation a resemblance to the way a physician speaks at the sick-bed; even if only medical experts understand it, it must never be forgotten that the situation is the bedside of the sick person."[7] Rather than regularly receiving the sacraments or attending church regularly, the goal of the Christian life is to become a person, a task much harder than it seems. While Kierkegaard does not yet make his critique explicit, it's clear that institutions more often hinder than facilitate such a task. The work of faith is strenuous, and it is singular. As he writes, "It is Christian heroism—a rarity, to be sure—to venture wholly to become oneself, an individual human being, this specific individual human being, alone before God, alone in this prodigious strenuousness and this prodigious responsibility."[8]

Aside from the critiques of institutionalism as such, *The Sickness Unto Death* contrasted sharply with the theology of Bishop Mynster, the head of the Danish church in Kierkegaard's time. The two men knew one another personally; the bishop had been friends with Kierkegaard's father and delivered the eulogy at his funeral. Kierkegaard also showed Mynster an early copy of the manuscript for *The Sickness Unto Death*, and the bishop tried unsuccessfully to dissuade him from publishing it. They also met after the publication of *Practice in Christianity* in 1850 and again clashed over critiques Mynster perceived in the text. Mynster was not the only personal connection Kierkegaard had to the Danish church; the man who replaced the bishop after his death, Hans Martensen, had taught Kierkegaard as a university student, and Kierkegaard's only surviving sibling, Peter, was a theologian of the church during Kierkegaard's lifetime and became a bishop following his brother's death.

Kierkegaard had long had a premonition that he would die young, and this fear turned out to be correct. On October 2, 1855, he collapsed on the street and was rushed to the hospital. He was lucid at the time, but his condition steadily worsened until he died on November 11. He remained committed to his anti-clerical principles during his long illness; he refused to see his brother due to his affiliation with the church and also would not take communion, as he viewed the priests as state functionaries rather than religious figures, rendering their conferral of the sacraments illegitimate. As the end neared, he requested to receive the last rites from a layperson, a request that was not met. After his death, the preferences of the living took over and he was accorded a traditional church funeral. One of his nephews, Henrik Lund, contested this verbally at the service, but his protests were ignored.

While Kierkegaard's attacks upon Christendom landed limply during his lifetime, they serve as a helpful road map for the virtue of refusal. So much of the anxiety we experience comes from the fear that things will remain forever as they are now, whether that is the individual worry that we will always struggle with sleep or self-image or larger concerns that the police will always play the same role in our society that they do at present. There is nothing to say that such things won't happen—no one can predict the future, as reassuring as that might be—but one of the ways to avoid giving into despair is simply to say "no." I believe police abolition is possible, and I choose to live in light of that fact and continue to work toward making it a reality. A common retort of critics to such demands goes like this: "What do we do with the rapists (or murderers, or child molesters, or other classes whose crimes make them social pariahs)?" While I believe there are good faith ways to address such concerns when they are genuine, most of the time those asking such questions do not really want an answer but instead want to point out the folly of imagining we could ever live without police, much in the same way we might seek to nullify the narrative of Abraham. Radical acts of imagination, whether the belief that you can hear the voice of God or the belief that we truly could abolish the police, always fly in the face of conventional wisdom to instead ground themselves in apocalyptic hope.

As a teenager, I was only dimly aware other expressions of Christianity beyond evangelicalism existed, and when such traditions were mentioned, it was usually to condemn them for how far they had fallen from the truth. While I never felt at home in the church we attended, every option presented to me seemed to be a variation of the same thing. I came to admire Kierkegaard's rebellious stance toward the Christendom of his day, and while the United States does not have a state church per se, the past few decades have illustrated the stranglehold white evangelicalism has upon American politics, a functional state church if there ever was one.

Now that I'm firmly lodged in one of those allegedly apostate traditions, Kierkegaard's attack upon Christendom no longer echoes within me in a such a deep way, yet I find myself returning to the underlying logic. The police murder of George Floyd in the summer of 2020 and the resulting uprisings across the world made clear to many that the police do not function to serve and protect but rather to, above all else, protect the interests of capital and enforce the brutal system of racial hierarchy that has been a part of American history from the start. At a protest I attended in my neighborhood in the summer of 2020, I saw it firsthand: when presented with a crowd pleading for their basic rights, the police formed a circle around the Akira clothing store on the corner.

The protests that happened in the wake of Floyd's murder were often organized around a central demand: defund the police. While many opinion writers and other professional pundits rejected such a call outright, they often did so by ignoring everything else that followed the initial demand. Defunding the police is the beginning; what accompanies such an initiative is the work of envisioning a world in which the police are obsolete, in which circles of mutual care and concern practice mutuality and restoration instead of punishment and incarceration. This requires us to imagine a future beyond the given one, much in the same way Kierkegaard sought to dismantle the religious edifice that dominated his day in favor of a radical encounter with a transcendent other. To hold onto such a vision of the future is a profound act of defiant hope, the reason for prison abolitionist and organizer Mariame Kaba's oft-repeated reminder, "hope is a discipline." There will always be voices suggesting we need to work at the margins, to make it a little less easy for the police to kill innocent people, often by giving them more money from budgets we are told are already strained. It is easy to forget that the police, like the state church of Kierkegaard's era, are both a modern invention and one of our own making. Police departments were created by our predecessors; they did not spring from the ground fully formed. To imagine a future beyond that which we can see in the present is a radical act, a gamble, but it can also be the answer to the pressing anxiety that fears things shall remain as they are indefinitely.

Yet something essential separates contemporary movements to defund the police from Kierkegaard's nineteenth-century attack upon Christendom. While the dominant biographical sketch of Kierkegaard as a lonely, awkward hermit owes more to contemporary satirical portraits from his interlocutors than his own life, he was indeed quite alone in his divorce from the religious institutions of his day. I felt this in my bones as an adolescent; my discomfort with my surrounding religious environment was something I locked deep inside, fearful of what might exist on the other side and feeling quite removed from everyone else around me. I know from experience how lonely and difficult this can be. Such isolation was at the core of much of the depression and anxiety I experienced at the time.

I'm not naive enough to think that such desolation has disappeared. There are assuredly those who have been radicalized by the events of the past few years across the country, but to hold such views in the midst of the Christian nationalism of the heartland in which I grew up is a lonely fate indeed.

I have wondered how I would respond to the events of the past few years if I were a few decades younger and still living in my hometown. I think I would be bothered and frustrated by them, much as I felt back then at the so-called war on terror and the war in Iraq. I would also most likely feel quite alone in those sentiments and experience some apocalyptic anxiety about existence as a result. We can't help where we start, but we can always help where we end up. In order to address anxiety on such an apocalyptic level, we need to be focused on building coalitions and organizing ourselves so that, together, we can dream of a better future. There is a certain romance in being the lone individual standing up to an evil institution, but this is seldom how real change happens. Kierkegaard may have done the best he could in an era where few wanted to hear what he had to say, but we are lucky enough to not live in such a moment. Due to the hard work of many who have come before us, a record number of people realize the systems we've created are profoundly broken and in need of change. Kierkegaard's thought helps us envision how to live in hope in historically uncertain and unhopeful times. I can think of no better remedy for the paralyzing anxiety that so many of us have been carrying. In the face of the seemingly inevitable march of state violence, we can together say: Christendom ended even though Kierkegaard did not live to see it, and police brutality and the prison industrial complex will end one day too.

CHAPTER 3

BECOMING HUMAN: MARTIN HEIDEGGER AND HANNAH ARENDT

My children remember the winter of 2022–23 as the one without snow. Both of them were born in the summer, but they love the winter—the snowmen and sledding and hot chocolate of it all. Every time it snowed that season, I watched as they attempted to build a snowman from the scant inch or so we received, making a figure that ended up being more mud than snow. Their sled sat unused in our basement storage. Their new snow pants remained in the closet. At first the lack of snow felt like a reprieve—no treacherous sidewalks, no tedious mornings cleaning the car windshield. But then it began to feel a little uncanny, and as the end of winter drew near without any real snowfall, it just felt sad.

I've been aware of climate change for most of my life, and I've seen and read various ways of conceptualizing the impact it will have upon the planet. I must admit I've spent quite a bit of time avoiding the issue, not out of disbelief but rather a willed ignorance. When I look at my children, though, I can't allow myself that luxury. I know their lives, and the rest of mine too, will be shaped in ways I cannot imagine by our ever-warming earth. They know little about the science of it now, but they can tell when something is wrong, when a winter comes and goes without snow.

My father's family is from northern Wisconsin, and each summer, we make a trip to see them and celebrate my grandmother's birthday. My grandfather was a dairy farmer, and though no one in the family farms anymore, several members still live on the acreage he worked when he was alive. On our most recent visit, my daughter was able to see and hold a small toad that was hopping amid the lawn chairs, and it electrified her. For the rest of our time there, she told us she wanted to move and live in Wisconsin when she grew up, that she thought the city was fine but that she would rather live amongst nature, that all animals were her friends. She also mentioned that maybe she didn't want to eat them anymore. I celebrated seeing her come alive, so vivid and so clear in her passion, but also felt a twinge of regret. What sort of nature, what sort of world, will be there for her once she grows up?

When it came time for me to choose a college, the clear choice seemed to be the University of Illinois at Urbana-Champaign. Once I arrived, though, it no longer seemed so obvious. Despite being in a city I loved, within an hour's drive of the home in which I grew up, I struggled with the transition. A therapist once asked me why I didn't dream bigger than my backyard, and while I didn't know the answer at the time, I've come to realize that the University of Illinois was the biggest place the frame I was raised with could accommodate. Out of a high school graduating class of forty-two, only two other students besides me went to four-year universities; the rest pursued community college, entered a trade, or started working. The University of Illinois, even if the distance wasn't far geographically, was located in a different universe from that. My parents had also divorced during my senior year in high school, and while it felt inevitable when it happened, it still shook me, making me feel vulnerable to sudden change in a way I hadn't before.

Once I moved on campus, I found myself drowning. In my first year, the undergraduate enrollment was over thirty-one thousand students; my entering class contained about fifteen times more people than my entire hometown. I struggled to connect, worried that I never would. I experienced more anxiety than I had at any point until then and probably since. I considered dropping out, transferring to a smaller, more manageable school. None of this resolved itself overnight, but gradually, I made friends—good friends who didn't merely tolerate or acknowledge my interests but shared them. By the end of my first year, I felt at home.

While my problems were resolved on an emotional level for the time being, left unanswered was the question of what I should study or aspire to as a career. I did not declare a major at first, thinking that perhaps some path would unveil itself to me, but I found that I was still the same person I'd always been. My English classes remained my favorite, so I declared that as my major, vaguely planning upon a future career as an academic or a writer. In my mind, that would allow me the opportunity to read as many books as possible and contribute in some way to a broader intellectual tradition. I found myself with extra time on my hands beyond the major and some prerequisites to fulfill, so later, I added a second major in philosophy.

I wouldn't say I was disappointed by the foundational classes I took within the philosophy department, but they didn't electrify me in the same way reading Kierkegaard did. Logic, ethics, the thought of Kant: all of it seemed important in the same way that having a healthy breakfast or following the schematics while building a piece of furniture from IKEA were. But none of it got to the big questions that occupied a not-insignificant part of my interior life. I continued to read outside of class—Kierkegaard as always but also those, like Camus and Sartre, who built upon his work in the existential tradition. Browsing the course listings for the fall semester one summer, I was excited to see there would be an entire class on Martin Heidegger, a thinker I knew was important but had never read.

I treasured those walks to class every Monday, Wednesday, and Friday. Alongside the main quad to the Gregory Building, the trees were aflame with all the colors of autumn. If I arrived early enough, I would encounter my professor at the back of the building, dispassionately holding a cigarette between his fingers. His entire personality seemed muted: clothes, tone of voice, facial expressions. In each class, we would pore over a few pages of Heidegger's most significant work, *Being and Time,* a thick black hardcover that took up most of the space in my backpack. My professor would unspool the text's marvelous compound words, full of hyphens, that I'm sure were more mellifluous in the original German. Even in their imperfect English equivalents, though, I found a new way to think about what it means to find yourself alive in the surrounding world and what to do with the sheer miracle of existence.

Being and Time, which was originally published in 1927, is dense and difficult; even with the aid of the class and subsequent rereadings, I'm not sure I entirely understand it. I feel okay with that; some texts aren't meant to be comprehended so much as they're meant to be experienced. Today, when I introduce my own students to some particularly dense psychoanalytic text, I assure them people have been debating for decades the precise meaning of what they are encountering for the first time—a century even, in the case of early Freud. I don't expect them to unlock it in a brief response, and in the same vein, I won't pretend to do justice to the whole of Heidegger's magnum opus here. Rather, I want to highlight what first stood out to me all those years ago, what lingers with me still, and how it might help us with the apocalyptic anxiety we may feel in our own time.

As his title suggests, Heidegger takes as his primary task the question of what it means to Be. By his account, this was the main question that concerned the Greeks and their philosophical pursuits, but we've largely abandoned it since then. "[The question of being] sustained the avid research of Plato and Aristotle but from then on ceased to be heard *as a thematic question of actual investigation*," he tells us.[1] It's not that subsequent philosophers have neglected the subject altogether, but the methods they've used to conduct their inquiry have failed to pierce to the heart of the matter. Most of the philosophical tradition has seen the issue as so evident it needs no further investigation, or conversely, impossible to answer, and both tendencies have crusted over the question of Being to the point that addressing it requires a lot of preliminary legwork, which is one of the reasons Heidegger's treatise is over four hundred pages long.

In a related vein, when philosophers have tackled the existence of objects in the world, they have done so at a remove, treating our relation to the world as if we were patrons at an art museum: looking, nodding appreciatively, watching, but not touching or using anything. For Heidegger, however, we encounter objects within a context, and they become most known to us not through idle observation of them but through use. "The act of hammering itself discovers the specific 'handiness' of the hammer," he writes. "No matter how keenly we just *look* at the 'outward appearance' of things constituted in one way or another, we cannot discover handiness."[2] In other words, the nature of our existence is to be in our surrounding world and make use of it, not as the isolated thinking individual of Descartes's "I think, therefore I am" but as someone who is an active participant in the life of the world and inextricably bound up with its objects. For this reason, Heidegger sets the goal of his inquiry as *Dasein*, a neologism usually left untranslated that means "being-there." To be is to be a part of the world. As I was learning to live beyond my anxiety and finding my own place in a world far bigger than I could have imagined, I found Heidegger's ideas about the nature of existence electrifying. To be is to live in a world saturated by possibility that we too often ignore; I cannot think of an idea more appealing to the undergraduate philosophy major.

I suppose it's no surprise that Heidegger resonated with me so deeply since I often did not feel like I was part of the world. I have worked with severely suicidal individuals. I have left sessions knowing I had no reason to recommend hospitalization, that I could not hospitalize someone forever, and yet I worried that they would not make it to our next session. I've never felt like that myself. I did spend more adolescent nights than I would like wondering if I wanted to wake up in the morning. I never had real plans to be the agent of my own destruction, but most of the time, I struggled to see a future for myself, to imagine myself being in the world. This might seem in conflict with the Christianity in which I was raised, and indeed I was taught and thought that suicide was wrong (albeit not a straight ticket to hell). It turns out, though, that believing God is always angry at you for your sins, sins which are all too easy to commit and that seem to pile on top of one another, and believing that same God will be returning soon to take away those who belong to him, leaving the rest to suffer tremendous torment, isn't a great motivation for feeling hopeful or invested in the future. Thoughts about the environment and global warming were not active concerns for me when I was growing up; the world was a place to escape from that would meet its end in due time regardless of our efforts.

Aside from perennial philosophical questions about what it means to be alive and to find oneself in the midst of the surrounding world, I find Heidegger's approach to be strangely hopeful. There is no shortage of things to make one cynical about the state of the world and the future of our species in it. Many elder millennials like me remember the buildup to the Iraq War that occurred in the early 2000s. I was not then and am not now a national security expert, but it seemed a strange leap to go from the war in Afghanistan, which seemed at least tangentially related to the September 11 attacks, to declaring war on a country that clearly had nothing to do with them. Various reasons were proffered at the time—all flimsy then and revealed to be entirely meritless soon afterward. Despite this, the overwhelming majority supported the war effort in the lead-up to the conflict, and while anti-war marches took place in major cities across the world, little of that sentiment filtered down to my small town in Illinois. The experience of the Iraq War and its aftermath left me and many of my generation feeling profoundly cynical about the United States and politics in general, and I suspect every generation in recent memory has such a watershed moment, whether it's Watergate, the Reagan "Revolution," or the election of Donald Trump. Cynicism becomes second nature in such fertile soil. This pervasive sense of doom is all too evident as well in contemporary conversations about the climate crisis. The point is not to replace knowing pessimism with blind optimism, though. We all find ourselves thrown, to use Heidegger's word, in a particular place and culture at a particular point in time, and we all try to make the best sense out of it we can. That process can bruise and sometimes break us.

Giving in to cynicism when faced with circumstances like climate change feels like a maneuver to repel a deep apocalyptic anxiety about the future: if I don't expect much from the world, I don't run the risk of being disappointed. I would suggest, however, that such cynicism often papers over a much deeper despair, a fear that even if I try to change the world or my surroundings, I might not succeed. This is seductive because it's logical to a degree; none of us can be sure our efforts will yield anything at all. To let this feeling overtake you, though, is to guarantee no change will happen. To be thrown into the world and to want to make it better requires a profound degree of hope. We cannot exist outside of the world as a Cartesian disembodied mind and think we can make much of a difference. To change the world, even by small degrees, requires us first to be in the world and to love it. Not to love the lies that led us to make war upon another country at great loss of life to that country's residents and our own soldiers, nor to love the resentment and racism that led to the election of Trump, but to believe that somehow despite all of that, a better future is possible. Heidegger reminds us that we exist in the world prior to any theorizing about it, and the attempt to recover this sense of initial connection can also be the impetus to work toward change at both the individual and structural level. While we are only talking about individual action in Heidegger's account, this can also provide the space needed for collective action as we turn toward each other and realize our apocalyptic anxiety is not ours alone.

That's easier said than done, however. Heidegger reminds us there are powerful forces working against our experiencing such epiphanies. Humans are unique among creatures in our ability to ask questions about the nature of Being, but we choose not to do so most, if not all, of the time, defaulting to lives of inauthenticity. As in Dostoevsky's parable of the Grand Inquisitor, most of us don't elect to utilize the freedom given to us, living instead submerged in what Heidegger calls the "they." The problem is not that others exist. Heidegger takes this as a given that we encounter other people in the same way we make use of objects in our world. This hammer belongs to Michael, who uses it for his job in carpentry; this field bounded by wildflowers is part of the property of Susan, who lives in that house. This Being-with is a fundamental component of our existence, yet it also means we tend toward living our lives in reference to others rather than grasping the inherent freedom that lies within reach of each of us: "We enjoy ourselves and have fun the way *they* enjoy themselves. We read, see, and judge literature and art the way *they* see and judge. But we also withdraw from the 'great mass' the way *they* withdraw, we find 'shocking' what *they* find shocking. The they, which is nothing definite and which all are, though not as a sum, prescribes the kind of being of everydayness."[3] We are used to thinking of our taste in music or art or the news we consume as part of the constellation of our personality, and while this is true, it is often far less unique than we make it out to be. I can remember the first time I heard some of my favorite musical artists, but while the discovery *felt* personal, it was always mediated by someone or something else: an online review, a music blog, a display at the store, a friend who knows a lot more about music than I do. Even if you only listen to Japanese noise or *musique concrete*, you almost aways encounter it through the mediation of another (who similarly heard of it from someone else, and so on and so forth), and part of the appeal of such obscurities is defying the tastes of the masses, preserving a protest connection to the they.

If this reminds you of Kierkegaard, you're on the right track. Heidegger retains much of the structure of the earlier philosopher's argument while rejecting the transcendent ground of being (i.e., God) Kierkegaard argues for.[4] While that difference is fundamental, the substance of Heidegger's argument remains the same: most of us swim in the sea that surrounds us without ever contemplating the nature of water. Like Kierkegaard, Heidegger sees the project of living authentically as one that can only really be approached by the individual.

If we do not have God to secure our sense of being and provide meaning, what does that leave us with?

According to Heidegger, to live authentically in the present means to live always facing the only future event we *can* guarantee will happen—our death. This is where the time portion of *Being and Time* enters. Evangelicalism had already taught me to live while keeping the end, both my own and that of the world, in mind, and while, by this point, I had rejected the transactional salvation I was taught as a child, I remained primed to consider this possibility as I moved through my existence. As Simon Critchley writes, "The self can only become what it truly is through the confrontation with death, by making a meaning out of our finitude. If our being is finite, then what it means to be human consists in grasping this finitude, in 'becoming who one is' in words of Nietzsche's that Heidegger liked to cite."[5] What helps us get to this point is something we've already encountered throughout this book: anxiety.

Heidegger isn't using the concept of anxiety in quite the same way modern psychology does, but he comes close. The sort of anxiety he writes about is what we would call generalized anxiety—that is, free-floating anxiety that's not attached to a particular object or person. As he defines it, "*That about which one has anxiety is being-in-the-world as such.*"[6] Whether or not you have experienced clinical anxiety, you probably have felt what Heidegger is talking about. Think about those late nights when you wonder whether or not you're living your life to the fullest, when everything you've done thus far seems like a shadow of what you once hoped to be. These moments of unveiling are difficult to be sure, but they can also be profoundly generative. By the time I encountered Heidegger, my anxiety had taken this form: I no longer worried about my impending damnation or particular concepts from the Bible but rather wrestled with the nature of what I wanted my life to be. If we embrace this anxiety, it can lead to genuine freedom. I have had more than a few patients who have experienced this dark night of the soul and emerged from it with a realization that they no longer wanted to finish their dissertation, that they should finally ask out that friend they have secretly had feelings for, or that they should make more time for themselves and reduce the role work plays in their lives. Knowledge of one's death is often intertwined with this, albeit unconsciously. Why stay miserable, knowing that we have a finite amount of time on this earth in which to seek out the best lives we can imagine for ourselves?

Death is guaranteed for all of us, yet it is the only experience we undergo that we cannot later describe to others. In arguing for the primacy of living with knowledge of our death, Heidegger isn't suggesting we live in fear and, by trying to avoid death, also avoid life. Nor is he saying we should dress in all black and only listen to the Cure (although freedom means we can choose that if we wish). Rather, he's suggesting that by accepting the end of our own individual being—that which can only belong to me—we are liberated from being sunk in the they and able to create a life worth living for ourselves.

Much of our politics is constructed around a denial of death.[7] We fail to take decisive action on climate change even as we annually suffer so-called once-in-a-lifetime severe weather events. We glorify the culture of youth and take steps to render ourselves forever young, whether through plastic surgery, inordinate exercise, or restrictive diets. Our own political system is a functional gerontocracy; Joe Biden became the oldest president ever upon his inauguration (at seventy-eight years old), removing his predecessor, Donald Trump (seventy years old at his inauguration in 2016) from occupying the top spot. We struggle on all levels, from the individual to the political, to cope with the fact of our own mortality and to live our lives in light of that fact. Acknowledging our common fate can help us avoid the denial that characterizes the life of the they and lend a real urgency to our work, but Heidegger doesn't get us all the way there. For the Heideggerian individual, the task of living authentically is always an individual and individualizing one. To surrender to the life of the community is our common lot but also the very condition for living inauthentically.

Authentic Being-towards-death can help us address existential anxiety—who I am, what I want my life to be like, what is most important to me—but can it point a way forward to curing the apocalyptic anxiety—about climate change, total political collapse, or global financial ruin—that permeates our lives? I think it ultimately fails upon this point. Heidegger's atomizing tendency in the face of wide-scale despair is all too prone to manipulation by those in power to minimize their role in the creation of the status quo and to distract us from pushing for systemic change. We cannot forget that the idea of a carbon footprint, one's personal contribution to climate change, is itself a creation of the fossil fuel industry. British Petroleum created a "carbon footprint calculator" in 2004 to allow each individual to tally their personal contribution to the earth's warming, thus shifting the focus from collective action to individual responsibility.[8] We each confront the anxieties of our age on our own, but the answer to our greatest fears lies in our shared struggle.

In my time studying philosophy as an undergraduate at U of I, we rarely considered the biographies of the people we were studying in any depth. We might talk a bit about the fact that Heidegger wrote *Being and Time* when he was thirty-seven and continued to build upon the book's themes in his later work, perhaps noting that his rural Catholic upbringing had some influence upon, say, his bucolic metaphors. What was never mentioned, though, was the fact that he was a Nazi. I have debated with myself when to bring this up in this book, and maybe at this point, it's too late, but I wanted to give this chapter the texture of my own relationship with Heidegger, his thought, and his betrayals.

Here are the facts as we know them: Heidegger became the rector of Freiburg University in 1933. Just a few days later, he joined the Nazi Party, three months after Hitler came to power and six years after the publication of *Being and Time.* He resigned from his role as rector the following year and expressed some dissatisfaction with the Nazi political program while remaining loyal to their ideals and maintaining his party membership. He was dismissed from teaching in 1945 upon the defeat of Germany and was banned from teaching until 1951. For the remainder of his life (he died in 1976) he never apologized for his involvement in Nazi politics or discussed it in depth.

The details of Heidegger's collaboration with the Nazis began to emerge a decade or so after his death, reaching their climax with the publication of the *Black Notebooks,* his collected private writings, in 2014. During his time as rector, he made several moves to align the university's administration more closely with the Nazis, denied financial aid to "non-Aryan" students, and informed on some of his academic peers whom he judged to be insufficiently loyal to National Socialism. He was not transparent in the years after the war, deleting comments praising the Nazis from lectures given at the time but published later, and destroying the copies of his notes that contained the original material. He resigned from the rectorate not out of principle but because he had alienated too many professors with his administrative decisions and no longer had their support.[9] The *Black Notebooks* further reveal not just his public actions but his private thoughts, which were suffused by anti-Semitism both before and after the war. Playing into crude stereotypes, Heidegger sees Jewish people in their supposed rootlessness as the antithesis of the specificity of Being, thus setting them up as paragons of inauthenticity—the enemies of authentic Being-in-the-world.[10]

Does this invalidate his work as a philosopher? *Being and Time* was written before Heidegger officially joined the Nazi Party, after all. While I would not call it a work of Nazi philosophy, it's clear Heidegger used the terms and concepts he established in it to make sense of the Nazi program. His devotion to German history and the German people was such that he saw their culture as capable of becoming a second Greece, and while he was never persuaded by the Nazis' racial reductionism, he believed they promised a revolution capable of breaking through the inauthenticity of the everyday and the politics of the Weimar era to offer a more authentic way of Being that would elevate the German people to the heights they deserved. Whether or not it is warranted, it's clear Heidegger himself thought the ideas advanced in *Being and Time* found at least their partial fulfillment in the Nazi project.

In wondering what to do with this or that problematic figure from the past, we too often ignore the voices we did not hear from because of the sins of these supposed "great men." The remarkable psychoanalyst Hans Loewald, for example, was a Jewish student of Heidegger, and I often think of the note he included in the preface to his *Papers on Psychoanalysis*: "Philosophy has been my first love. I gladly affirm its influence on my way of thinking while being wary of the peculiar excesses a philosophical bent tends to entail. My teacher in this field was Martin Heidegger, and I am deeply grateful for what I learned from him, despite his most hurtful betrayal in the Nazi era, which alienated me from him permanently."[11] Heidegger's reprehensible politics caused Loewald to abandon academic philosophy entirely, and while philosophy's loss was psychoanalysis's gain, I can't help but wonder how many other voices were silenced by Heidegger's betrayal and never heard from again.

Around the same time I was reading *Being and Time*, I also began devouring academic theology. Upon the recommendation of my college pastor, I bought *The Politics of Jesus*, by the Mennonite ethicist John Howard Yoder, which offered a strongly pacifist reading of Jesus's life and ministry and called contemporary Christians to better embody the radical politics inherent in his mission.

I devoured everything I could find by Yoder and some of his students; my move toward leftist politics owes much to what I absorbed from those writers. A few years after I encountered Yoder, the Anabaptist Mennonite Biblical Seminary apologized for covering up his history of sexual abuse, harassment, and assault of more than fifty women. By the time they apologized, Yoder had been dead for seventeen years. The facts were there if I had looked closely, but few were obvious at the time; his books were published widely by respected Christian academic publishing houses in the years following his death; his works were cited frequently by those disciples I had learned so much from, even though many of them knew in detail about his history of rape and sexual assault and his attempts to justify it theologically; and few seemed willing to touch the history of violence committed by a man so outwardly devoted to peace. I will be disentangling my own thoughts about Yoder's theology and ethics for the rest of my life, a small price to pay indeed in comparison to the scores of women he abused without remorse. When someone is offering a theory for what the good life should look like and we later find out their own life falls miserably short of their lofty ambitions, it can and should call their project into question.

The fact that Heidegger was a Nazi and remained unrepentant about that fact until the end is beyond dispute. What is left to us is to determine what we do with his thought from here. I don't think his work in *Being and Time* is irredeemable, but I do think we can find traces of his later Nazi turn within it, and indeed within any politics that centers our certain demise above all else. Thinking about one's impending death has a long tradition in various world religions, from the *memento mori* tradition found in Judaism and Christianity to forms of Buddhist meditation that encourage the practitioner to envision their moldering corpse. These practices, though, occur within traditions that both make sense of death within the tenets of the faith and give it some significance or meaning. While I don't think this is a necessary condition—consider Mary Oliver's "Tell me, what is it you plan to do / with your one wild and precious life?" as a sort of secular manifesto of the same—lacking a ground in the transcendent, however one chooses to define it, can yield anxiety instead of quelling it.[12] In the end, Heidegger isn't able to shed Kierkegaard as he hoped.

I'm thinking here not just of the kind of anxiety that might make one extra fearful to cross the street or visit a neighborhood the media portrays as "crime-ridden" but an anxiety that one's way of life is disappearing. There is a short road indeed from this latter sort of anxiety to taking drastic, often selfish actions to try to preserve one's cherished traditions. One of the paths of radicalization for modern white supremacy is a concern that whiteness is somehow threatened by the rise of tolerance of racial and other minorities. This need not take the form of mass shootings and neo-Nazi death cults, although it can. It's also reflected in the rise of efforts to ensure white children will never have to learn about or reflect upon the role of white supremacy in structuring modern society. Feeling like one's way of life is slipping away can cause us to seek to find new modes of being, but it can also cause us to cling tightly to the vestiges of the old and fight against any attempts to modernize or adapt. A politics structured around our impending end may be value-neutral on its face, yet it can often induce drastic actions to try to avoid death in its various manifestations. Heidegger's Nazi politics were rooted in this, and so are modern expressions of white supremacy and other forms of hate. This does not negate the liberation one might feel from realizing we have one short life to live, but it does underline the need to look for a more secure base upon which to collectively confront our anxieties about the future of our world and our common life. If a politics of death doesn't fully get us there, would a politics of life? If so, what would that look like?

Following the 2016 election of Donald Trump, one could observe the way people coped with their disbelief by monitoring the bestseller lists. One book frequently cited as an answer to the question "how could this happen here?" was Hannah Arendt's *The Origins of Totalitarianism* (1951). Arendt needed no such renewed relevance to secure her legacy; her examination of the factors leading to the rise of Nazism and Stalinism has often been cited as one of the most important books of political theory of the twentieth century. As a German Jewish woman who witnessed the rise of Hitler and was forced to flee her native country, her interest in the topic is obvious, but I wonder if her status as a former student of Martin Heidegger helped further prod her theorizing in this direction.

Arendt first encountered Heidegger when she was an eighteen-year-old university student and he was her thirty-five-year-old professor. They began a four-year romantic affair, but while a married professor with two children having a relationship with a pupil half his age is a gross betrayal of the student-teacher relationship no matter how you approach it, Arendt doesn't describe it that way. They drifted apart for a few decades during the war, but Arendt weighed in on Heidegger's behalf once he tried to return to teaching, painting his Nazi dalliance as an act born of naivete instead of malice, and they remained close friends until Arendt's death in 1975.

Arendt's thinking is multifaceted and encompasses a wide variety of interests, reflecting the peripatetic nature of her teaching career, which eschewed tenure-track positions in favor of shorter engagements at a variety of prestigious institutions, including the University of

Chicago. Most agree that her major contribution to philosophy is *The Human Condition* (1958), and for our purposes, I'm most interested in her concept of natality, which she explores throughout that work. By natality, Arendt means the fact that we live in a world that is continually welcoming new humans into it, that a Being-towards-life is one of the fundamental features of our politics. With its connotations of birth and renewal, natality isn't intended as a direct response to Heidegger's Being-towards-death, but I believe Arendt gets us closer to that which would liberate us from the apocalyptic anxiety of our age.

Arendt opens *The Human Condition* with a bit of awe streaked with suspicion: "In 1957, an earth-born object made by man was launched into the universe, where for some weeks it circled the earth according to the same laws of gravitation that swing and keep in motion the celestial bodies—the sun, the moon, and the stars."[13] The launch of *Sputnik I*, to Arendt, was an event "second in importance to no other, not even to the splitting of the atom," and it marks the long-gestating ascension of science atop all other disciplines. Arendt grasped in her time that which has only accelerated in our own, as the humanities have continually eroded within the halls of academia. In all of these scientific advances, though, Arendt sees a denial of that which makes us most human, whether it be the hope to leave our earth behind to settle elsewhere or other attempts to defeat our oldest foe, death, and live forever. These questions, she notes, are not scientific but political, and it is a mark of the decline of political thought that they are not seen as such by the vast majority of people. Against such willful ignorance, she states her thesis: "What I propose, therefore, is very simple: it is nothing more than to think what we are doing."[14] What we are doing, then, is the *vita activa,* the active life, which Arendt believes has been too long ignored by the Christian tradition's emphasis on the *vita contemplativa,* the contemplative life. The *vita activa* is marked by three essential tasks: labor, the tasks we must accomplish to sustain everyday life; work, effort directed at a defined end point that results in a tangible good; and action, the sphere in which we interact with others and come to know both them and ourselves.

Arendt sees each task as being part of what makes us essentially human and oriented toward not just individuals' survival but the endurance of the species—that is, each of them is a *political* act. Labor, work, and action are all rooted in natality "in so far as they have the task to provide and preserve the world for, to foresee and reckon with, the constant influx of newcomers who are born into the world as strangers."[15] Of the three, action is most closely intertwined with natality because part of being born into the world is the ability to remake it into something different. Therefore, since "action is the political activity par excellence, natality, and not mortality, may be the central category of political, as distinguished from metaphysical, thought."[16] The fact that people are always being born and becoming potential change agents in the world we create lends the political project an element of hope. But it also gives it an undeniable air of frailty.

Heidegger proposes we see the future as foreclosed by our own death and that we work to wrest meaning from it. Arendt questions the individualistic notion of such a concept, for in her telling, part of what makes us human is the fact that we live in and form communities. It is those communities, and not merely our singular lives within them, that are the locus of change and hope. She proposes this with reference to the Greek philosophical tradition, the same one Heidegger believed had the courage to address the questions of Being that had been abdicated by those who followed. Arendt doesn't confront Heidegger directly in *The Human Condition,* but were we to set their works in direct conversation, I believe she would remind him he is telling only part of the story. The Greeks didn't tackle questions of Being in isolation; rather, they formed schools to interrogate such questions together, and the metaphysics that so interested them cannot be divorced from the politics they believed was the communal expression of the nature of the universe. The Greeks' democratic experiments—and they were indeed experiments because they did not go far enough in assigning liberty to truly everyone (and the American founders who loved them would repeat this error)—were inextricably bound up with their philosophical endeavors. In this way, then, Arendt is the philosopher who exercises the most fidelity to their principles, even if their concept of democracy would have excluded her.

Natality can be overwhelming as well as hopeful; the fact that people are always being born into a world with a rapidly changing environment makes addressing climate change far more urgent. I can sometimes delude myself that I will be able to navigate the uncertainties of the future, but my bravado evaporates when I consider the world my children will be forced to inherit. Even if you don't elect to have children of your own, the sheer natality of the world remains, and it's no better to consign others to doom just because they do not happen to share your DNA. But there's hope here if we let it breathe. Those in power love to position older and younger generations against one another, whether it's stories about how millennials like myself ruined the housing market and who knows how many other things with our addictions to avocado toast and lattes, or how Gen Z's obsession with the latest TikTok trend or K-pop band means they have abandoned the things that count. Real hope, though, can only be accomplished via cross-generational solidarity, and that is the surest way out of the apocalyptic anxiety that plagues us when we turn toward the future. The future's radical openness can only be addressed together.

This sort of solidarity must do more than just transcend generational lines. As I wrote this chapter, news reports detailed how a third of Pakistan was underwater due to heavy flooding and how the entirety of Puerto Rico lost power due to a hurricane. I fear that just a few years from now, as such events become near-weekly occurrences, these facts will say little to date the composition of this book. No community is spared the effects of global climate change—and wildfires in the American West are quite happy to consume the homes of the rich and powerful—yet the effects of broad-scale environmental degradation are already being felt most keenly by those left out of contemporary systems of power, and these inequalities will only grow more pronounced in the coming years. The politics of natality reminds us to be open to the potential of new birth—not just of the children who look like us or share our country of origin but the wild possibilities inherent in humankind as a whole. We must work against our ingrained prejudices and preferences to ensure a better future for everyone if we truly want to prioritize life over death.

Many of us exist in regular community only with those who are already like us: our coworkers make the same amount of money we do; our friends usually share our income level and interests; and in dating, we tend to unconsciously gravitate toward people from our own social and economic class. Solidarity that transcends the ties we too often use to divide ourselves is the only path forward in a rapidly changing world. The future is open only if we let it be; if we give in, the politics of death that defines our gerontocracy will continue. No amount of merely reading or thinking about it will suffice. If we are to make it, or perhaps even thrive, we need each other.

CHAPTER 4

THE GOLDEN MEAN: ARISTOTLE AND ALASDAIR MACINTYRE

In September 2018, my job sent me to a conference, a rarity in community health, where margins are thin and expenses must be kept to a minimum. For two days, I sat in a large conference room in Milwaukee and heard from some of the best minds in the field regarding the treatment of trauma. Influential mental health professionals offered densely footnoted lectures that providers like me discussed at small tables, about how to bring trauma-informed care to the populations we serve. The conference happened to take place during the second round of testimony determining whether or not Brett Kavanaugh would be confirmed to a seat on the Supreme Court. During breaks in our day, I would hurry back to my hotel room to watch Christine Blasey Ford testify about her alleged assault at Kavanaugh's hands when the two of them were in high school. It was hard not to see the parallels between what we were discussing and the impact the violence Blasey Ford described had upon her life. It was also difficult not to hear the disbelief and denial of Kavanaugh and his defenders as an echo of what occurs with frightening regularity in homes, emergency rooms, police stations, and courtrooms across the country. I left with some practical tools for helping our patient population who survive trauma, along with a deep concern that those in power fail to take such concerns seriously, thus ensuring the steady transmission of pain and suffering across generations.

Kavanaugh was confirmed, of course, as was Neil Gorsuch before him and Amy Coney Barrett after. Thus it happened that a president who lost the popular vote by nearly three million votes was able to remake the Supreme Court in a radically conservative direction. I am not starry-eyed about the supposed neutrality of the highest court in the land; I was in high school when five justices handed the presidency to George W. Bush. Any serious study of the past reveals a history of decisions that later people will judge harshly, from the well-known to the more obscure but no less detrimental. Regardless, it is clear that the Supreme Court as it's currently constituted has an overwhelmingly conservative majority, and that has had dire consequences for some of the freedoms and rights we hold most dear. In just the past few years, abortion rights have been decimated, affirmative action ended, and a right for private businesses to discriminate against queer people has been upheld, to name just a few nauseating developments. The Supreme Court can feel unimpeachable, and it's clear that some of the justices feel they are indeed above all laws or ethical codes. And while there seem to be some options for dealing with such an ideological runaway court, all of them require a creativity and a conviction that most in the liberal establishment seem to lack. Are we doomed to feel a pit in our stomachs each June as the court's term ends and more decisions limiting our rights and remaking our country trickle out and slowly erode that which we once thought was certain?

As I progressed through my undergrad program, it became clear that my dream of a career in academia was far from settled. The higher education job market has only worsened in the years since I graduated with my bachelor's in 2008, but the writing was on the wall even then. The commencement speaker for the English Department that year was an alumna who had migrated to the business world, and she assured us that such a move could be ours too if we wanted it. I found the idea offensive at the time—the university had a school of business already, one I eschewed in my choice of major—but I can appreciate the efforts she made, however feeble, to assure us we had career options available to us beyond the stereotypical path of barista or bookstore employee. I didn't let it bother me too much, though, because by that point, my plans were settled in an altogether different direction.

I didn't feel confident about where I fit in faith-wise upon arriving at college, but I didn't yet have it in me to break with the long-standing tradition of attending church on Sunday mornings. The fear of getting it wrong with eternal damnation in the balance was less keen but still present. With a few of my friends, I began attending a small campus church that combined students and members of the community in roughly equal proportions. The pastor had a PhD in history and taught and wrote in addition to his pastoral duties, offering a model for taking faith seriously but not blindly. The services had a structure to them, a faint hint of liturgy that, compared with the freewheeling Pentecostal services I'd been raised with, felt as high church as the Latin Mass. Before I had encountered any of this for myself, though, I knew the church was on the same block where I lived and had services that started at 11 a.m., two factors that won me over before I set foot through the door.

The pastor recognized something in me and worked to get me more involved in the life of the church, asking me to volunteer in various capacities, including leading book studies examining popular theological works alongside other members of the congregation. I hadn't dabbled in serious theology beyond some of the popular works I'd read to retain a semblance of faith when I felt like I was drowning, but I quickly discovered many of the things that drew me to philosophy only seemed to take on greater urgency when God was the object of their consideration. I still felt out of step with the evangelicalism in which I was raised, but while my college church held many of the same beliefs, the way in which they wielded them felt different. I began to think it might be possible to stay within that camp while migrating to a more moderate, considered position. I even thought I could help lead this charge by working within church leadership. My doubts about faith had grown quieter. My anxiety faded as I began to feel like I was meeting myself for the first time. I even sometimes liked what I saw.

I decided to go to seminary after graduation, the same one in the Chicago suburbs that my pastor had attended. I didn't have a fully formed idea of what I wanted to do, but I thought the balance he struck between service in a local congregation and academia was appealing, and I hoped I could emulate it. One of my college friends had accepted a job with an engineering firm and bought a house a short distance from the school, so I moved in with him and started my graduate studies. So began three years of intellectual and personal formation that would put me in a markedly different place from where I'd started.

I found myself particularly interested in a field called political theology, which, in short, investigates the ways our beliefs shape our sense of community and points us toward where and how the church should be active in the world. As I moved through college during

George W. Bush's second term as president, I began to feel that I could not afford to remain on the sidelines. I had noticed for some time that Jesus had very little to say about many of the features of modern life that most animated evangelicalism—namely gay people, sex, and abortion—but he had a whole lot to say about the poor and how they are (mis)treated. We also don't get to choose what first awakens us to a different reality, so I must confess I was also an ardent U2 fan at the time and wanted to replicate Bono's mixture of religious devotion and political sincerity. I hoped through academics to address the nagging need to do more to help the world around me, and if I emulated a certain Irishman in the process, that would be okay with me too.

Lurking forever in my head, though, was the basic question of whether or not I was a good person. When I was feeling calm, responding to that question was an intellectual exercise. When my emotions were a tempest, it was an urgent matter requiring an answer at once. Such a query is familiar to many with anxiety and depression, the nagging fear that perhaps the requisite social niceties are papering over some unique form of evil within. In my life, evangelicalism helped contribute to this muddy morass. The message I had received upon this subject while growing up was decidedly mixed; my parents were broadly supportive of me, and I didn't get into anything resembling trouble in high school, but I was also taught humans were sinful from the very beginning and deserving of hell from the moment they entered the world. The ethical content, if you could call it that, of the churches I attended growing up still centered upon prohibitions, different somewhat in scope from the fundamentalism of my earliest memories but still obsessed with what one was *not* to do. Abiding by the rules wasn't difficult for me, but I didn't know what to do with the time that was left. What did it look like to be good? Such a question seemed essential to the political theology project I imagined for myself, and the answer something I needed to help me sleep at night. As always, the personal and the academic were deeply intertwined.

In the meantime, I was devouring all the theology I could find, consulting with one professor in particular as I shaped my own intellectual interests in addition to the material I was covering in class. There was a hunger within me I have rarely felt since, and while my life was not particularly balanced at the time between my intellectual, social, and personal interests, in hindsight, this was undoubtedly one of the formative periods of my life. I found what felt like an answer to the question of how to be good by going back, way back to the ancient Greeks—Aristotle in particular.

Aristotle hadn't interested me much in my undergraduate years, beyond a vague historical curiosity in the development of philosophy, but when I was in seminary, I encountered a variety of thinkers who argued his contributions to ethics remained unsurpassed, if neglected in the present. I don't think it's impossible to approach someone so ancient and so influential as Aristotle without bias, so I would never contend my reading is "the" right one, but within his thought and the later uses made of it, I found something resembling an answer to that fundamental question I'd been asking myself.

Aristotle's major contribution to ethical thought is his *Nicomachean Ethics*, titled after his father and/or son, both of whom were named Nicomachus. There is only so much one can know about something so ancient, but the text we have today is based on lectures Aristotle gave to his school of philosophy. Dating its composition is difficult; it was probably composed during the later stages of Aristotle's career, before his death in 322 BCE. The *Ethics* is connected with another of his "practical" works, the *Politics*, in that both are concerned with the shape of the good life, and to be good in Aristotle's reckoning is to be an active participant in the life of civil society.

In Aristotle's view, the goal of both a life well-lived and of politics is *eudaimonia*. This is often translated as "happiness," and while that is literally correct, the type of happiness connoted by the term is far more robust than the way in which I might say my morning coffee or a good session with a client makes me feel happy. Happiness in the popular sense is a reaction to the present moment, but the type of happiness Aristotle describes is only possible within the scope of a lifetime. *Eudaimonia* is the end toward which humans strive, and achieving it means fulfilling the purpose of our species. An excellent hammer drives nails in cleanly and with minimal effort; an excellent human has *eudaimonia*. Unlike with hammers, however, what it takes to reach that sense of excellence is a matter of some debate. This sort of happiness isn't something one can aim at directly, as so many self-help books promise to do, but is the result of the well-lived—that is, virtuous—life. All of this takes time—a lifetime, in fact. As Aristotle writes, "For one swallow does not make a spring, nor does one day. And in this way, one day or a short time does not make someone blessed and happy either."[1] Now that we feel sufficiently overwhelmed, where do we start?

The operating concept in Aristotle's ethics is balance, often called "the golden mean." As he defines it, "Virtue is concerned with passions and actions, in which the excess is in error and the deficiency is blamed; but the middle term is praised and guides one correctly, and both [praise and correct guidance] belong to virtue. Virtue, therefore, is a certain mean, since it, at any rate, is skillful in aiming at the middle term."[2] Consider what it means to be courageous—perhaps not the first place we would turn to in a consideration of how to live but one of the core virtues in Aristotle's scheme of the good life. If you were walking down the street and saw someone being mugged, what would you do? You could, for example, turn, run away, and never mention it to anyone. While this might be an understandable reaction, few would consider it an ethical decision. Aristotle considers running away from the feared object or encounter to be an example of cowardice. But neither would the sensible person rush headlong at the mugger, not stopping even when he trains his firearm upon you. This polar opposite of cowardice is recklessness, and it also isn't very helpful to your ethical development (or to the person being mugged). To be virtuous requires acting somewhere in between these options, attempting to help the person being mugged but in a level-headed way, perhaps by calling for help, making your presence known, or offering aid. Throughout Aristotle's discussion of various virtues, he counsels us to take this middle road—don't throw away all your money but don't hoard it either; don't be excessively prideful or self-abnegating; have a healthy degree of ambition without descending into either megalomania or laziness.

Before reading Aristotle, I had never thought of living in such a way. Throughout my childhood and adolescence, I heard stories of people who prayed for hours every day, or who moved abroad to become missionaries on what seemed to be the thinnest of pretexts. For most of my childhood, I had a nagging fear that one day, I would feel God calling me to do the same and I'd have to live the rest of my life in a foreign country, fulfilling a predetermined call in which I had no say. I had never encountered the thought that one could try to live sensibly and, in that, to be living rightly.

But I can't just blame evangelicalism for this imbalance in which I lived; when it seems like the world is falling apart around you, balance can seem suspect, selfish even. If the Supreme Court is eroding our democracy piecemeal, shouldn't we be calling our senators every day, volunteering for campaigns every cycle? Perhaps. That course of action isn't wrong, of course, but it's also not very sustainable for the majority of us. If I devoted myself fully to such tasks, I wouldn't be a very good husband, father, or therapist, and doing these tasks well is also part of making the world better.

The concept of self-care was obviously foreign to Aristotle, but the golden mean serves as an important reminder that we can only help the world if we are still around to do the helping. Working within the field of social work as both a practitioner and an educator, I have seen many driven, passionate individuals aflame with a desire to change the world, and I have also seen them crash against the rocks of a society that seems not to care, institutions that don't have their backs, and a profession that often prefers to tinker at the margins rather than work to implement real, structural change. The answer is not to abandon such desires to change and confront systems of inequity—I would hate to live in a world where this was the case—but to temper that drive with an honest assessment of how difficult such change can be, and to develop practices that can help sustain us as we wait.

For a majority of the history of philosophy, Aristotle's position on ethics was the default, if not the only, one. When Thomas Aquinas set out to write his definitive account of Christian thought in the thirteenth century, he based his own ethics upon Aristotle's; he's so central to Aquinas's *Summa Theologiae* that he is simply credited as "the Philosopher." More recently, however, Aristotle's approach, usually called virtue ethics, has often been supplanted by either the deontological or consequentialist approach. The deontological school of ethics is often associated with Immanuel Kant, whom we encountered earlier in our discussion of Kierkegaard, and his idea that the ultimate criterion by which we can judge whether something is right or wrong is whether or not we would elect to make such a decision a universal rule. So, when confronted with the mugger, I should act as I would want the rest of humankind to do when facing the same situation. Rather than focusing on the decisional element, the consequentialist (also known as utilitarian) school of ethics says I should be focused on what I foresee as the best possible outcome. Thus, I might consider whether or not the mugger has a weapon, consider the various ways in which such an encounter might end, and decide that the most ethical thing to do would be to stay back and keep my distance. None of these three approaches may look that different in everyday practice, but they are each premised upon quite different notions of what the good is, how I should consider myself in relation to others, and what the role of other people is in the calculus I make while trying to decide how to act.

Enlightenment thinkers like Kant developed their ethical systems in opposition to Aristotle. We need not let this ancient Greek dictate what is right and wrong in our own age of universal rationality, the logic went. Editions of the *Nicomachean Ethics* often contain a table of the various virtues Aristotle discusses alongside their various mutations, and nothing could seem more suspect in an era that prized the faculty of logic freely gifted to "everyone" (usually meaning wealthy white men, of course) than the idea that a single person was the authority upon what to do or to avoid in a given situation. Against Aristotle's communitarian ethos, ethics of the past few centuries has almost always focused on the rational deliberations of the individual. We can see this logic at work in the construction of the Supreme Court, created by founders who were in thrall to Enlightenment thinkers like Kant: a handful of appointed and august jurors weigh pressing debates of the day against the principles established by the Constitution to determine whether or not various rights and responsibilities are due to every American citizen. I doubt it has ever worked that way, at least in a sustained manner, but the decisions of the past few decades strain this ideal past the breaking point. Even those who take their side cannot, and usually do not, argue that Alito, Thomas, and the other conservative justices are impartially calling balls and strikes; their appeal lies in the "wins" they've established due to the conservative takeover of the court.

Virtue ethics never really went away (the extent to which it has been utilized by Aquinas and other theologians ensured it remained the standard within theology, especially of the Catholic variety), but it did lose its luster. I would suggest, though, that it has wider applicability beyond dogmatic debates in an era in which those who are supposed to be some of the final arbiters of reason appear captive to special interests and demonstrate little interest in the ethical life. In the recent past, a few notable thinkers have tried to resurrect the virtues—chief among them, the Catholic philosopher Alasdair MacIntyre. It is through his landmark *After Virtue* that I first began to reconsider the idea of virtue ethics, and I find myself returning to it in the face of the radicalized Supreme Court.

MacIntyre begins *After Virtue* with a thought exercise: "Imagine that the natural sciences were to suffer the effects of a catastrophe. A series of environmental disasters are blamed by the general public on the scientists. Widespread riots occur, laboratories are burnt down, physicists are lynched, books and instruments are destroyed."[3] We might still possess the vocabulary of the scientists, and we may be able to refer to concepts such as "mass" or "gravity" with some accuracy, but we would not be able to weave them together within the tapestry the natural sciences have established. Even if we could still recall that gravity is what causes an object to fall to the ground once I let it slip from my fingers, if we're unable to describe the complex interplay between gravity and other forces that makes up the world as we know it, something would be forever lost. Even philosophy wouldn't be able to help us, for it all too often skims along on the surface of the given; it might be able to note these lacunae, but on its own, it could not fill them. We would be living in a world drained of much of what makes it meaningful or life-giving, with few options for reawakening such impulses within us. This, MacIntyre suggests, is precisely what has happened if we swap out "natural sciences" for "morality."

I imagine the "M-word" gives some readers a shiver. Today, we most often talk of Supreme Court justices and their partisans trying to legislate morality through overturning abortion and the like, binding the many to the particular ethical code of the few. And, as is so often the case, those most concerned with making other people live under their moral code have little interest in binding themselves to the same precepts, as the numerous ethical shortcomings the court demonstrate. MacIntyre is not suggesting such sweeping enforcement of particular norms or values, although like most ethical systems, the virtues can be bent to serve both conservative and progressive ends. Rather, what this little thought experiment is meant to show is that with the decline of virtue ethics, we have lost the ability to give an account to one another of what the good life is and how to best live it. One need only pull up Twitter (or X, or whatever it may be called at the moment) and witness the ceaseless arguing past each other of people who share the same ideological core commitments to see that MacIntyre has a point. What sets virtue ethics apart is not a list of particular dos and don'ts—even though Aristotle offers something like this in the *Nicomachean Ethics*—but the perspective it offers. What matters in a particular situation is not whether I want my actions to be universalized or if the outcome is the best possible one for the largest number of people. What matters is how my actions make me a certain kind of person.

Virtue ethics gives us back the narrative of our lives. The *Iliad,* the works of Aristotle, the Christian New Testament, the works of medieval philosophers and theologians—they all differ in the qualities and practices they emphasize or downplay, but they all share a core conviction that to live rightly is to live a goal-directed life to achieve the flourishing of humanity. What ultimately makes a life well-lived is the sort of story it tells. We achieve this through what MacIntyre calls "practices," defined as "any coherent and complex form of socially established cooperative human activity through which goods internal to that form of activity are realized in the course of trying to achieve those standards of excellence which are appropriate to, and partially definitive of, that form of activity, with the result that human powers to achieve excellence, and human conceptions of the ends and goods involved, are systematically extended."[4] A practice enables us to live a meaningful life in which we feel we contribute to the well-being of ourselves and those around us.

In MacIntyre's account, this includes rule-bound activities such as chess or football, vocations like farming, and disciplines like architecture, music, or engineering. A practice contains internal rules that help us judge whether someone is practicing well or not—chess pieces move in certain ways and the game is over at a defined point—and some sense of achievement, whether it's the satisfaction of a game well played, a building, or a new composition. Practices also occur within a historical narrative. What I consider to be a praiseworthy example of architecture may not have been so to the ancient Greeks, but I did not arrive at that conclusion on my own. Even if I prefer the most avant-garde of styles, this came from somewhere and is part of a historical lineage. The virtues, then, are what it takes for practices to succeed.

To not disappear further into abstraction, consider my own field of psychotherapy. Psychotherapy is a practice governed by certain norms—what we call the "frame." If you try to find a new therapist for yourself, you may look for someone who specializes in a particular condition or takes a particular approach, but regardless of whether that person is trained in the treatment of trauma or not, uses cognitive behavioral therapy or family systems theory, is located in the downtown of a major city or the outskirts of a rural area, when you go in for a session, you will expect to talk about yourself to someone whose job it is to mostly listen, offer supportive feedback, and keep the focus upon you rather than upon themselves. This is therapy's "frame," the way the practice has been done well since its very beginning. To do these things, then, is *part* of being a virtuous therapist.

Thus far, we've primarily been considering what not do, of course: talk excessively about oneself, charge burdensome fees, attempt to initiate romantic relationships with patients. One can avoid all of these prohibitions, though, and still not be effective. Social workers have a code of ethics like many other disciplines, and while following them might make you an ethical therapist, it won't necessarily make you a good one. You can know the rules of chess intimately and still play a boring game that doesn't go anywhere if you don't attempt to capture the opponent's pieces and place his king in checkmate. Playing in this manner fails to satisfy the latter part of MacIntyre's definition of a practice, the element of trying to achieve a standard of excellence. It is necessary but not sufficient to follow the rules; you have to try to get somewhere. This can be easier said than done when it comes to the messy stuff of human lives, yet there is an important kernel of truth here as we seek to live when it feels like we're approaching the end of the world. Facts alone do little to motivate people toward change; if you watch the news, you will be able to rattle off the never-ending parade of Supreme Court cases stripping our rights away, but that knowledge alone rarely incites one to act. If we want to change the world as it exists, we have to not just express our condemnation of how it looks right now but offer an alternative vision for where we want it to go.

This leads us to the problem with so much of our ethical talk these days: it remains focused upon what one should not do—whether that is having premarital sex or using the wrong vocabulary—and it lacks a suitably thick account of what makes a life good. Many have remarked with wonder how evangelicals can claim to have so many moral convictions while demanding almost nothing of their preferred political candidates when they don't appear to follow them, but considered from the perspective of an ethical system focused only upon prohibitions, that isn't all that surprising. Generations have been raised being taught solely what not to do, so it shouldn't be remarkable that so many seem to lack any sense or conviction about how to best live one's life.

We often cling to a version of the ethical life that is only premised upon what not to do because it offers a sense of safety at the expense of freedom. To be an ethical agent in the world invests our actions with a gravity that is both welcome and dizzying. When I decided to pursue becoming a clinical social worker, I felt a sense of excitement at the future possibilities but also a healthy sense of dread at the responsibility. A particularly beloved professor of mine named Stanley McCracken helped address this fear by confronting it head-on, assuring us that this was a hard field we were entering and it would probably take five to ten years before we were very good at it. Keep in mind the acronym CHERS, he told us: if you act with compassion, humility, empathy, respect, and sensitivity, you may not be able to help everyone you meet, but you won't make their problems worse. That might seem like a small reassurance, yet it has stuck with me all these years.

Each of us is embedded with a series of practices; I am simultaneously a therapist, husband, father, progressive, and Christian, among other things. To be considered truly virtuous, however, requires acting as a whole, integrated person. We could certainly conceive of someone who is a fantastic therapist, patient and kind to his clients, forgiving of their faults and mistakes, but who fails to reflect such characteristics toward his spouse or children. The history of psychoanalysis provides us with plentiful such examples. MacIntyre is not suggesting such people do not exist, only that their lives are not intelligible as virtuous, even if they have the outward appearance of being so.

All of this, of course, requires more work of us than, say, basing our ethics upon the decisions one makes in a particular moment in time without much regard for what comes before or after, but this complexity matches the reality of our lives. All of us are embodied within various traditions that shape our decisions and determine what it means to be ethical. This includes the histories in which we happen to find ourselves through an accident of birth. I have certain responsibilities as a white American who has benefited in ways both known and unknown from this country's legacy of white supremacy. Declaring this as part of my narrative doesn't clarify how to act in light of that fact, but it does mean that any serious consideration of how to live must include the forces that have brought each of us to the place we are at now alongside a vision for how to remake the world anew. This also resists the atomizing tendency present in so many of our fears, forcing us to consider both the historical legacies we bear and the hope that communal action can form a different way of being upon the bones of the old.

Such considerations are foreign not only to the way we usually speak of the ethical life but to therapeutic approaches to change as well. If there is one thing any approach to therapy must have, it is a road map for how to behave differently within a given situation, but as I noted at the outset, much of the therapeutic language around behavior fails to match the needs of our current cultural moment. The cognitive and behavioral traditions that dominate social work and counseling degree programs utilize the metaphor of a triangle, the three sides being made up of emotions, thoughts, and behaviors. Intervene upon any one of them, the theory goes, and the other two will follow. If you feel so depressed that you can't get out of bed, push yourself to do so and your emotions should improve. If you feel overwhelmed by anxiety, try to confront your fears instead of running away from them and notice how your thoughts lessen in intensity. This isn't sufficient for confronting apocalyptic, culture-wide anxiety, but I also don't think it does an adequate job of capturing human behavior even when it comes to more manageable concerns. These models reduce us to a sort of machine, altering inputs for a different output and vice versa. This reductive approach to what it means to be human is only possible in a time that has evacuated the virtues of meaning, leaving us to marinate in our anxieties about the future even if we manage to pick up a few breathing techniques or cognitive reframing suggestions along the way.

Consider an example from an essay on the virtues by Iris Murdoch, a novelist and philosopher also steeped in the tradition of the ancient Greeks.[5] A mother, M, finds herself not altogether fond of the woman, D, whom her son marries. M recognizes D has a good heart but is lacking in some social refinement and seems rather immature. Being a good mother, M does not give her son any indication that she thinks he has married beneath him, and she is nothing but kind to D. The drama here is entirely internal; if we plotted it along the cognitive-behavioral triangle, only one side would be engaged. I imagine this situation is all too familiar to most of us—we don't get to choose our family, our work colleagues, or the people our children bring home, and there are times we might find ourselves not connecting with someone on a personal basis, though we still strive to remain warm toward them because we know that is the sort of person we want to be.

M, however, is not content to remain in her disappointment. She loves her son and trusts him, so she works at loving D, seeing her actions in the best possible light. And, given time, this works. There are many different ways to interpret M's actions—she could be deluding herself, revisiting her opinions about what constitutes proper behavior, learning to see D differently the more time she spends with her, or some combination of the above—but no one could deny that something profound has happened within M, even if accounts that reduce humans solely to behavior cannot make sense of it. There is nothing exotic or far-fetched about Murdoch's account; in fact, similar things happen to most of us all the time. There are certain romantic comedies that my wife enjoys and revisits often. I had not considered myself a fan of romantic comedies before we met, and when we first watched them, I mostly agreed because it made her happy. This was no great sacrifice on my part, to be clear, just what it means to share a life with someone. Over time, though, I became more open to them, and while I can't say I love them in the same way she does, I enjoy them and look forward to our annual fall rewatching of *When Harry Met Sally.* Something has changed for me.

Humans are ineluctably more complex than our ethical or psychological theories can encompass. Approaches that seek to distill our complexity into easily manageable bites may reduce anxiety in the short term, but may also come at a very high cost, requiring us to forsake some of that which makes us most human and alive to the moment. The strength of both virtue ethics and psychoanalysis in their own registers is not the fact that they manage to answer such questions but rather that they leave space for them in their unanswerability. As we confront the challenges of our future, we should ask ourselves not what we should do in any singular situation but rather what sort of person—and people—we want to be. There are moments in life we attain such clarity, but without a framework for making sufficient sense of it, such moments are always in danger of collapsing.

This perspective also helps us cope with the possible defeat of our efforts. No matter how hard we try, it's possible our democracy could fail to outlive us through some combination of electoral defeats and Supreme Court decisions. This is a sobering thought, but while we might make every attempt to avoid such a possibility, we are only one instrument within the symphony of history. Even in the collapse of meaning, however, we can still live a life worth living. This is, in fact, what countless people in other times and countries have been doing since time began. Returning to the practices that sustain us gives us meaning even in the worst of times but also saves us from the nihilism that can result from such disappointment. The future is and remains unwritten, despite all the seeming certainties of the present.

My time in seminary was both immensely rewarding and intensely lonely. Between my classes and the reading I was doing on the side, I discovered just how narrow was the tradition in which I had been raised. For the first time, I read deeply outside evangelicalism, and I discovered I had far more in common with those voices than the ones I had been taught were my own. I began a process of transformation that would see me finally leave evangelicalism behind, culminating in my confirmation in the Episcopal Church six years after I graduated.

Such a transformation did wonders for my religious anxiety but also wreaked havoc upon my life plans. When I began my first year of studies, I intended to move back to Champaign-Urbana for my second year to intern under my college pastor and commute to my classes. It took me most of the first year to realize I had no interest in doing that. By the time I finally made up my mind to withdraw, I had already packed up my belongings to move out of my friend's house and let someone else move in. I called my former pastor, told him I couldn't do it, then couch-surfed for a few months while I figured out how to salvage my life and my seminary career. I deferred my internship for a year, found a therapist, and moved in with some classmates.

I never really found the sort of community at seminary I hoped I might, the sort that MacIntyre and others think is necessary to sustain one and enable one to live virtuously. The lofty rhetoric I was reading didn't match up to my reality. Other changes had occurred of which I was unaware. The nature of theological education had changed over the previous decades. I was an anomaly—most people deciding to enter ministry were doing so as a second career. A cluster of other students, about ten to twenty, lived on campus at any given time, but the vast majority commuted to evening classes after a full day's work and went back home the moment they were over. They were all nice enough, to be sure, but they had their own lives. I did not.

My path away from evangelicalism felt like mine alone. I received what I consider to be a fairly good education; no one pretended the earth was created in six days or denied there were elements of the Biblical texts that existed in tension with one another. The seminary I attended worked hard to take the middle path. They had a long tradition of supporting women in ministry, and while I often forget now that this was and is an issue for many, I appreciated their openness. They were less open to the idea of LGBTQ people in ministry—that was banned according to the student handbook. We mostly didn't talk about that, but I couldn't forget about it. What had been something that crossed my mind occasionally became a question I could no longer ignore, and while I didn't hide the fact that I became affirming, I didn't feel like I could broadcast it either because that could bar me from graduating. So I put my head down, kept working, and hoped to attend a PhD program in a more open environment.

Since I had grown confused about where I fit into the larger Christian landscape, ministry no longer felt like an immediate career path for me. I planned to defer that for the time being and confront it later, once I was safely ensconced in a PhD program. I did everything I could to become an attractive applicant. I took classes at other theological institutions throughout the Chicago area, regularly overriding the cap on the amount of courses I was allowed to take. One semester saw me in classes from 9 a.m. until 10 p.m. with a few breaks to eat and commute, and while that was exhausting, it also filled me with energy. I felt like I was finally moving toward the future I wanted. I served as a TA to a professor and also interned at his church. We worked on a book project together about the future of evangelicalism, and while he ended it with a call toward reform, the process only helped solidify my intention to leave it all behind.

I had been lonely in other ways over the course of my time in seminary. I had dated little in my undergrad years—not for lack of trying—and I hoped that once I knew myself better, that would improve. I was dismayed to discover the median age of my classmates was around forty, and while I was lucky to find work at a local church a few weeks after beginning the semester, the congregation was small and older, which made me feel stuck. I became convinced I would be alone forever in a way that only someone in their early twenties can. My therapist encouraged me to try online dating, but that was before it had reached the level of social acceptability it has now, and I couldn't bring myself to do it. To me it felt like giving up. It didn't help that most of my peers, both those I knew from college and my seminary classmates, were married or in serious relationships. Looking back, I probably felt most alone during those years, and as my anxiety receded, I found depression taking its place.

I began to feel hopeful in the winter of my final year, when a girl I had met two years before sent me a message out of the blue. By this point, my PhD applications were in, and I was waiting to hear back while looking forward to graduating. We fell into a relationship quickly and deeply. It didn't sting that much when I received rejections from the two schools I most wanted to attend.

My backup accepted me, but the prospect of moving away no longer seemed appealing. I decided to defer that decision. The girl I was dating offered to get me a job at the same organic grocery store where she worked, and while part of me thought the work was beneath my graduate-level education, the idea of taking a break and working for a year in a job altogether removed from that which had consumed me for the past three years seemed appealing. She had PhD aspirations as well, so together, we decided to try again in a year.

Even though my life didn't look as I had planned, if you had asked me, I would have said I was living the good life, a virtuous life, to the best of my abilities. I had someone I cared about and imagined we could erect a life together. Community is not a good in itself, however; plenty of people find a sense of belonging amongst others who share their prejudices of one sort or another or stay with people who don't have their best interests at heart for fear of what the world might look like without them. I did not find myself sucked into any such social movement, but I had placed my trust and, with that, my vision of happiness in someone who did not deserve it, was not capable of holding it for me. I do not think my prior beliefs and priorities were wrong, but when that relationship crashed down around me, I felt unmoored, unsure of what it meant to be happy. These feelings, difficult though they were, led me down a far different path both professionally and romantically.

CHAPTER 5

THIS FILTHY, ROTTEN SYSTEM: JANE ADDAMS AND DOROTHY DAY

There are some purchases I will always associate with the pandemic, things we bought to make our indoor lives less miserable. The cheap digital projector that enabled us to have movie nights snuggled up in our bed. The wooden climbing triangle our kids used to burn off energy when the playgrounds were closed. The Instant Pot that made mealtimes easier while my wife and I were both trying to balance working from home with taking care of our kids. The Instant Pot had been out for a decade at that point, so we were late converts, but it helped make our lives and the lives of millions of others easier at a time when we would take whatever we could get. It surprised me when the company, which had become so ubiquitous, filed for bankruptcy in 2023, but while I appreciate what our Instant Pot has contributed to our lives, especially during times of stress, I didn't exactly shed tears at its demise. Beyond the future of one convenient appliance, however, the "failure" of the Instant Pot is a case study in the excesses of late-stage capitalism, the economic system we have inherited and that continues to wreak havoc in our lives in all sorts of ways, both big and small.

As Amanda Mull wrote in the *Atlantic,* part of the problem with the Instant Pot is that it is too good at its job: "A device developed primarily to address a particular food-prep inefficiency has a natural ceiling to its potential market, and when one catches on as quickly and widely as the Instant Pot, it can meet that market ceiling in pretty short order."[1] Sales figures reflected this; in the past few years, sales of appliances like the Instant Pot dropped by half. The real downfall of the device, however, began earlier, with the company's acquisition by a private equity firm in 2019. The features that made it appealing to consumers rendered it uncertain as a profit-generating machine: Instant Pots tend to be reliable, and there weren't many new and flashy improvements that would convince people to upgrade every few years. The firm that bought it attempted to expand the Instant Pot name into other kitchen appliances, but these met with little success. So, once they had drained their acquisition of any value, they dumped it by filing for bankruptcy.

The downfall of the Instant Pot was disappointing news to me, but the extractive dynamics embodied by private equity concern me far more when they're extended to sectors meant to benefit everyone, such as journalism, entertainment, transportation, and the internet. We see how private equity's strategies play out daily in the dearth of local news options, which has fueled the rise of misinformation and opinion masquerading as objectivity, the gradual erosion of new and interesting entertainment in favor of endless retreads of existing intellectual property, and the dismantling of once-crucial platforms like Twitter. Such changes have decimated entire sectors of the workforce and transformed others from stable careers to random sectors of the gig economy.

Not everyone has been hurt by such changes, however. The average pay of CEOs has risen 1,460 percent since 1978. In 2021, CEOs were, on average, paid 399 times as much as a typical worker within their company.[2] Wages have exploded at the top and stagnated at the bottom, leaving millennials and younger generations without the ability to financially plan for the future, if we are even able to plan for our present. It's important to acknowledge as well that while more and more people are being locked out of financial stability, that has never been a possibility for far too many Black and Indigenous folks and other people of color who have to live in a country stratified by white supremacy.

How do you plan a life within a system that seems aligned against you? How are you supposed to play a game that seems like it's been rigged for generations? You can try to work from within the system, scraping what you can from it. I think about the college students I see who end up pursuing consulting or finance, even if the work itself leaves them unmoved and uninterested, because they've been told it is the best path to financial stability. I cannot blame them for worrying about having enough money to provide for themselves or their families, but I mourn the lack of choices extended to younger generations. Accommodation is not the only option, however. One can also question the right of the system—built as it is upon exploitation and inequality—to even exist in the first place.

A year after I graduated from seminary, I found myself still working at a grocery store, single, and without a prospect of beginning a PhD program. It had taken a few months after graduation for my relationship to fall apart, and when it did, I felt like my life was over. I found myself stuck in a job that had felt acceptable as a transitional stage alongside someone else but was a sign of utter defeat on its own. I was just managing to scrape by on my hourly work, scanning the work schedule as it was released each week to ensure I had enough hours to pay my bills. Usually I did, but sometimes I didn't.

I wasn't reading much of any significance during this time, preferring to spend my time away from work numbing myself with television. After a few months of this, I resubmitted applications for PhD programs without a sense of what I might do if they didn't work out. I didn't get into any of the schools I wanted to, and the program I previously deferred no longer had a spot for me. I had pinned my last hopes on that option, trying to convince myself it was what I wanted. When my mother texted to tell me my rejection letter had arrived, I was at work. I crouched down in the tiny prep kitchen amidst the samples and cried.

I thought long and hard about whether or not I wanted to continue my efforts. As I did so, I recalled the PhD students I had met during my various campus visits. They were doing interesting work and seemed like people I would like to spend time with, but most of them were quite open about the despair they felt at their job prospects. Many were raised evangelical like me, no longer felt that way, and didn't know what lay on the other side of their original commitments. There was a persistent fear that you could think yourself out of a job, either through evolving in a way that no longer let you sign the statement of faith required by so many colleges as a condition of employment or through producing work that didn't pass the test of evangelical rigor. Given my intellectual interests and my evolving faith, I knew I would not be exempted from such considerations.

I know now, in a way I didn't then, that attending seminary is not a typical on-ramp for a PhD program; a master of divinity from a seminary is a practical degree to prepare one for ministry, not a preparatory degree for research. My college pastor was the exception rather than the rule. There may have been other reasons I wasn't admitted—I cannot claim to know the answer—but it dawned on me that no amount of trying would necessarily yield the result I wanted. There are one-year master's degrees that can serve as a transition between seminaries and more rigorous PhD programs, but I began to feel like I was done trying. I had not lost my faith—that would have made the matter more convenient. My faith life had changed, and while I briefly considered pursuing ordination in the Episcopal tradition, a few Google searches and a conversation with my then priest revealed that could take some years to happen. I was deeply unhappy and knew I couldn't wait that long.

I tried to return to the roots of my thinking, teasing out the values that had made the life of an academic so attractive. I had been drawn to theology because I thought it could help make the world a better place. I wanted to highlight the way our faith commitments could and should help shape the way we live in the world. In a roundabout way, I was trying to offer a different, more holistic vision of what faithful engagement with the world might look like, to try to address the gaps and fissures that had stirred up my anxiety since my adolescence. Instead of seeing the world as a place full of sin, due to be abandoned by the truly faithful any minute in the rapture, I wanted to share the hope I had found with others and, in so doing, help them avoid some of the pain and anxieties I had experienced. My brief experience of low-wage work had further radicalized my politics, and I wanted to do something more than write about it.

The process of moving on was gradual. There was some mourning involved but also a sense of hope that I might finally find the meaning I had been looking for. I found taking charge of my future and weighing the options in a serious way helped lift the fog I'd been operating under for so long and reduced the 3 a.m. rushes of anxiety about what I was doing, or failing to do, with my life. While in seminary, I interned on the West Side of Chicago and found my work with recovering addicts the most rewarding experience of the pastoral work I did for my degree. I had known social workers, both as my own therapists and in my social life, and I admired the work they did, the flexibility of the degree, and the profession's commitment to social justice. I decided to join them and returned to school for a very different sort of education.

I recall a moment after I was accepted to the University of Chicago's School of Social Work Administration (later renamed the Crown Family School of Social Work, Policy, and Practice), the school I would attend and at which I now teach. It was an early morning shift at the grocery store just a few months before I would be able to leave for good. I had been there since 5 a.m., breaking down pallets of milk and fruit. I stole away for a minute to go downstairs and use the restroom, and doing so reminded me of all the times when I had needed a moment alone there to quell my anxiety over the future or cry over my failed relationship. Catching a glimpse of myself in the mirror, I realized I looked different. I looked happy.

While I was in seminary, there was a certain poster that accompanied me everywhere I lived. My decorating standards were less rigorous than they are now, and I would usually thumbtack it above my desk. It depicted an older white woman sitting with her legs crossed, stony-faced and serious. She is flanked on either side by police officers, their guns and nightclubs in the foreground of the picture. Beneath it is a quote from the woman, the Catholic activist Dorothy Day: "Our problems stem from our acceptance of this filthy, rotten system." Although I knew little of Day when I first bought the poster, I appreciated her work as the founder of the Catholic Worker Movement and admired the sentiment. Once my time in seminary was over and my interest in academic theology began to wane as my distance from it grew, I became more curious about her life and what it might offer as an example for living out one's convictions.

Day's most popular work is her 1952 autobiography, *The Long Loneliness*, and like many, I first encountered her writing there. Day wrote the book in midlife to provide an account for her first conversion to radical politics, her subsequent conversion to Catholicism, and later, her founding of the Catholic Worker Movement alongside Peter Maurin. The organization began as a newspaper—befitting Day's previous career as a journalist, first for leftist outlets and then for Catholic publications—and developed into a movement with houses of hospitality scattered across the United States and the world.

Reading *The Long Loneliness*, I was struck most by the lack of a clear conversion experience in Day's narrative: she holds the same values and core convictions from early in her life and finds different ways to express them as experience and knowledge guide her further into (and out of) herself. As a child and adolescent, Day was profoundly religious in a way that was out of step with her family. She shares a letter she wrote to a friend at fifteen: "I have so much work to do to overcome my sins. I am working always, always on guard, praying without ceasing to overcome all physical sensations and be purely spiritual. … Oh, surely it is a continual strife and my spirit is weary."[3] Day left to attend college at the University of Illinois, my own alma mater, the following year and began to lose her interest in religion: "But that time was past. I felt so intensely alive that the importance of the here and now absorbed me. The radicalism which I absorbed from *The Day Book* and Jack London, from Upton Sinclair and from the sight of poverty was in conflict with religion, which preached peace and meekness and joy."[4] For a time, Day shed her youthful piety to labor for the salvation of the masses from the forces of capitalism. She left the University of Illinois after two years and moved to New York City to write for a series of socialist publications. Her peripatetic activism reflects someone wrestling with the injustices of the world—the miseries of the systems humans have created and maintained—while striving to find a community and a cause worth fighting for. Reflecting upon her struggles to find a place where she belonged is a welcome reminder that every age has to confront their own apocalypses and work to wrest meaning and freedom from them in the midst of struggle.

Day not only wrote about but participated in protests around progressive causes of the day, spending fifteen days in jail following an action for women's suffrage. She encountered many of the prominent leftist voices of her time and had a string of unsatisfying romantic affairs. She finally found what felt like happiness with a biologist, Forster Batterham, and they lived together in relative bliss for a few years as unmarried partners. Day's religious yearnings never entirely left her, but Forster, a staunch materialist, remained uninterested. This remained a slight but noticeable tension within their relationship until Day discovered she was pregnant. She decided she wanted to keep the baby and have her baptized into the Catholic Church, both of which Forster opposed. She and her daughter, Tamar, became

Catholic, the relationship ended, and the life of Dorothy Day, Catholic activist, began.

For a while, Day did pretty much the same sorts of things she did before her conversion—she wrote, attended protests, and wrote about attending protests—but this time for Catholic publications, not socialist ones. She believed Catholicism offered a robust theology of work and the rights of all people, but she was dismayed that most leftists and most Catholics didn't seem to realize how the two could and should inform each other. After returning home from covering a protest in Washington, DC, she discovered a French itinerant named Peter Maurin, who had been told by one of her editors to look her up. I can't imagine returning from a grueling trip and being hospitable toward a stranger my roommate had let into my kitchen, but they bonded quickly. Together, they agreed to form a newspaper they called the *Catholic Worker*, riffing off the Communist *Daily Worker*. In the *Catholic Worker*, they merged Maurin's philosophy of "cult, culture, and cultivation" with Day's journalistic interests, and they expanded their shared vision into a house of hospitality in New York that was open to all, and a series of farms run as communes. Reflecting upon her life up to the time of its publication (*The Long Loneliness* was released when she was fifty-five), Day realized she had found what she had been seeking from her youthful wanderings: "We have all known the long loneliness and we have learned that the only solution is love and that love comes with community."[5] The *Catholic Worker* became the answer Day had been striving for without even knowing it.

I find the Day of *The Long Loneliness* admirable but also somewhat alien. Throughout the book, she seems to operate with a certainty and conviction that I can approximate only on my best days. She retains her fiery commitment to the struggle to make the world a more just place alongside a profoundly spiritual core that finally found its fulfillment through founding the *Catholic Worker*. In some sense, this problem plagues all conversion stories, with their need to establish a narrative unity over the messiness of one's life such that it naturally culminates in the realization of some truth or condition without pretending it could ever be otherwise. My Dorothy Day poster followed me around for a time as an example of an idealism I could admire but not really hope to approach myself.

Once I was accepted to graduate school for social work, I began to think more deeply about the connections between my faith and my newfound field, and in the Catholic Worker Movement, I saw clear parallels to the settlement house movement of Jane Addams and others that birthed the discipline of social work. My own graduate institution, the University of Chicago's School of Social Service Administration, was founded by Addams's colleagues. Wanting to dig deeper in Day's life, I picked up a volume of her diary entries, *The Duty of Delight,* and encountered a different perspective on her life.

Day began her diary in 1934, the year after she founded the *Catholic Worker*, and she continued it in fits and starts until her death in 1980. The chronicle of her life that spans these pages echoed far more with my own experiences and gave me a deeper appreciation for her life and work. The immediacy of the diary transcends some of the artifice of her more conventional autobiographies, and she sounds refreshingly human. She struggles to find time for herself and feels guilty when she does: "These hours on train or bus are so precious—to be alone for a short while, it is a complete relaxation, a joy. I am a weak and faulty vessel to be freighted with so valuable a message as cargo."[6] She reports frankly on the misery, perhaps even depression, she experiences: "My nights are always in sadness and desolation and it seems as tho as soon as I lie down I am on a rack of bitterness and pain."[7] She wonders what she is doing writing while so many others are in pain: "The world is too much with me in the Catholic Worker. The world is suffering and dying. I am not suffering and dying in the CW. I am writing and talking about it."[8] She asks herself if all the work is worth it: "So often one is overcome with a tragic sense of the meaninglessness of our lives—patience, patience, and the very word means suffering."[9] There is never enough money to be had, and personal squabbles between members of the various houses and communes threaten to overtake the mission. Alongside these entries exist the facts of her life, that despite wondering if the work was worth it, sometimes being quite convinced that it was not, she carried on and did not waver. Seeing just a glimmer of her inner turmoil gave me a much deeper appreciation for all that she accomplished.

And what she accomplished was indeed profound. Today, there remain 178 Catholic Worker communities scattered across the world, each autonomous but devoted to the vision of working with those marginalized by society in the struggle to build a better future. The Catholic Worker houses are connected to the same settlement house movement that gave birth to social work, but there are some essential differences that have made Day's legacy endure into the twenty-first century, even as Jane Addams's Hull House is now a historical site. Some of this is generational; Hull House was founded eight years before Day was born. Their differing visions about how to most help those left behind by society, though, played a larger role in determining which vision would last longer. Settlement houses were largely locations where people from more privileged backgrounds came to live amongst the (usually immigrant) poor to attempt to help them while also conducting research to bring their plight to a wider audience. While contemporary social work looks quite different, it has not entirely left this dynamic behind. In learning about and thinking through the history of social work alongside Day's work,

I developed a vision for what I wanted my practice to look like and where I hoped my own field, and by extension our world, could be headed.

The Catholic Worker included privileged people, to be certain, but Day's vision was to provide not just a center that community people could visit but also a place with room for everyone. Her diaries testify to how difficult this could be to maintain, how many struggles came from bringing such disparate people together under one roof, but she wanted the Catholic Worker houses to always be houses of hospitality. In many ways, her vision was less grandiose, more measured, than that of the early social workers, and in that, she was able to attain a balance they often lacked.

The history of charity work is marked by people of privilege parachuting into poor communities, offering some help, and then returning back to the safety of their familiar surroundings to share what they saw. Day believed the poor were where Christ could be found, and she viewed living and struggling with them as part of her vocation. Settlement houses included an element of community uplift as part of their programming: they offered the equivalent of adult education classes and other vocational and educational programs to the immigrant poor. This is an undeniable good in the abstract, yet an element of coercion and control can easily slip in the back door. Such programs all too easily become training in how to be American, how to assimilate. This critique was made at the time by radicals such as Emma Goldman, who remarked that settlement work was "teaching the poor to eat with a fork." The work of the Catholic Worker, by contrast, was mostly focused upon presence; they served meals to the poor in their communities and farmed as a means to continue this work but did not view their mission through the lens of social uplift. In Day's anarchic vision, there is no place to be uplifted to because there is nothing deficient in the poor but rather in the society that makes them poor and ensures they stay that way. Settlement work sought to train those at society's margins to better fit within its boundaries, while the Catholic Worker Movement challenged the very existence of a society that could declare some in and others out, opting to abstain from participation in such a system and seeking, instead, to dismantle it.

These tensions have been present from the very beginnings of the practice of social work. In their recent paper "To 'Elevate, Humanize, Christianize, Americanize': Social Work, White Supremacy, and the Americanization Movement, 1880–1930," Yoosun Park and Michael Reisch locate social work within the broader practice of Americanization around the turn of the twentieth century as the United States emerged from the Civil War with a new zeal for integrating immigrants into the country, usually by stripping them of any vestiges of their homeland and native practices.[10] Settlement houses were just one cog in a vast social machine that sought to Americanize these "foreigners"; other places that offered such vocational programming included employers like the Ford Motor Company, various chambers of commerce, church groups, and patriotic organizations like the American Legion, the YMCA, and the YWCA, which all sought to assimilate immigrants into the American project. These processes also created and maintained racial supremacy by flattening the differences used to distinguish various European national and ethnic groups to subsume them under the unifying concept of whiteness. These new Americans thus became enlisted in the struggle to maintain racial order in the face of groups racialized as "other," such as Black Americans, Latinx people, Asians, and Native Americans. Through a rigorous study of primary materials, Park and Reisch illustrate how rather than countering such voices, social work participated in practices that erased difference and promulgated a particular white, Christian, and middle-class view of what it meant to be an American. As the Americanization movement faded and was replaced with a more militant anti-immigrant rhetoric that has continued to our own day, the social work profession transitioned from what Park and Reisch call the coercive to the maternalistic, yet "social work's conviction about the rightness of the white, middle-class, Anglo-Nordic standard remained intact."[11]

Even today social work continues to wrestle to vacate this conviction. Most social workers are white; many of the people we work with are not. In our own era, this often takes the shape of white social workers leaving their neighborhoods and communities to offer services (therapy, case management, and so forth) in less-advantaged communities with a distinctly different racial composition. The poor pay associated with such work often attracts a more economically privileged class that can afford to forgo some material benefits, either due to family largesse or the salary of a partner, for the sake of the job. Much of this work can still take the form of coercion and control, despite all our talk of social work values and emphasizing the "person in the environment." Social work as a profession is not as far removed from pursuits like finance, consulting, and private equity as we might hope; all in their own way seek to uphold existing structures and keep them intact.

Consider child protective services, perhaps the first thing that comes to mind when most people think of social work. When we think about child protective services, most of us think of case workers removing children from homes where they are at imminent risk of harm due to physical or sexual abuse. While this makes up a percentage of cases, it's far from the majority. According to data gathered in 2017, 75 percent of CPS cases were due to neglect; sexual abuse made up 9 percent, and physical abuse was 18 percent. The percentage of cases due to neglect jumped a full twenty-six percentage points from 49 percent in 1990. What do we mean by neglect? According to the Department of Children and Family Services of my home state, Illinois, neglect is "the failure of a parent or caretaker to meet 'minimal parenting' standards for providing adequate supervision, food, clothing, medical care, shelter or other basic needs."[12] While some parents may do this out of malevolence, the vast majority of them want to take care of their children. Neglect occurs when a parent is unable to do this due to financial circumstances or a knowledge gap, neither of which can be adequately addressed from within the carceral logic of child protective services. The system of child protective services we have inherited is meant to discipline and punish those who would hurt children, not help those who want to be good parents but lack the means to do so. It is no coincidence that as the economy began to work less for more and more people, the proportion of neglect cases skyrocketed. Further accelerating this trend was the welfare reform movement of the 1990s, which saw fewer parents qualify for benefits and limited the amount and extent of help available for those who managed to receive some aid. There is also a vast racial disparity at play, which has to do with what kind of parents we view as needing help versus those we criminalize. The history of social work demonstrates how easily those in power are able to assimilate some degree of critique—in this case, that children aren't being properly cared for—and make some gesture at establishing equity while leaving the larger structures of society in place and ensuring that existing power dynamics are not disturbed. This sounds sinister, but I don't think many of the original architects of the child protective system were evil. Rather, they were, and still are, participants in a society structured by white supremacy and capitalism that saw certain types of parents as being inherently more worthy of respect than others, and they built structures that upheld these values rather than doing the harder work of self-examination and liberation.

These racial dynamics extend to who gets to become a social worker. I am now licensed to independently practice social work, but that didn't happen immediately upon graduation. Once I received my master's degree, I had to work under the direct supervision of a licensed clinical social worker, meeting weekly to discuss cases and my approach to the practice. This takes most social workers around two years to complete, depending upon the nature of their work and the particular requirements of their state. Once I met these requirements, I applied to take an exam developed by the Association of Social Work Boards (ASWB). After passing, I received official confirmation that I could now practice independently. Licensure matters for a few reasons. It denotes that someone has taken the work seriously and has continued to develop their style and skills after graduation. It is meant to assure that everyone who practices clinical social work (i.e., works in the mental health field) has a certain level of knowledge. Beyond these more idealistic reasons, it also matters to insurance companies and thus to employers. Private insurance companies will only pay for therapy services delivered by a licensed professional who is either providing the services or, in some cases, signing off on each service offered by a pre-licensed supervisee. This makes licensed clinicians attractive to employers because they require less work to supervise and they bring in higher rates of pay than public insurances (i.e., Medicaid and the like), which allow for interns and pre-licensed professionals to provide therapy.

For years, there have been questions about the pass rate of the ASWB exam, particularly when it comes to the race of the test-taker. Many noticed Black social workers in particular struggled to pass at the same rate as their peers, even when accounting for things like graduating from the same program. The ASWB resisted releasing any data on the pass rate until, under mounting pressure, they finally caved in 2022. The data proved what many had long assumed. For the clinical exam between 2018 and 2021, the pass rate was 91 percent for white students, 77 percent for Latinx students, and only 57 percent for Black students. To introduce a bit more clarity into the data, consider only test-takers from my alma mater, the University of Chicago. Depending upon where the rankings fall in a particular year, the

University of Chicago is among the top three schools of social work in the country, so there should be no question that the education one receives there should suffice to pass the exam. The pass rate for white students reflects this at 93 percent; yet the pass rate for Black students is a full twenty points lower.[13]

When it comes to the particular problems that plague society, a common refrain is to add more social workers to the situation. Are police killing too many people with mental illness when responding to 911 calls? Replace them with social workers. Struggling to deal with a sense of crippling anxiety about your future? Talk to a therapist. Concerned about that neighborhood child you fear isn't being adequately cared for by their parents? Call in the social workers of child protective services. I find some of these policies to be promising and others to be suspect, yet beyond the implications of, say, establishing a mental health crisis line to dial instead of relying upon 911, we need to think about who exactly we are proposing to replace the police with. I was drawn to the field of social work because of its stated goal to work to establish social justice, yet while these efforts at equality are realized occasionally, it remains an oft-elusive dream in the same way democracy has been within the American experiment. The solutions we propose to the problems that haunt us too often leave existing power structures intact while agitating for small changes around the margins.

Social workers are not vested with the power to wield violence without repercussions within our society—that belongs to the police. Of course we should send mental health workers to aid people experiencing a mental health crisis, just as we would call a plumber and not an electrician if our toilet won't stop running. At the same time, though, we should ask ourselves how that person ended up in a crisis. Social workers should all become abolitionists, working to envision a world in which our services are no longer needed. Is the person able to access insurance to afford the therapy or medication they might need? Do they have supports available to them, familial or otherwise, to help them deescalate before they reach a crisis point? Are their basic needs being met? If we do not ask ourselves these questions, we are doing the bare minimum, keeping people alive (and our consciences clear) while doing little to make the lives of people experiencing mental illness tangibly better. We are merely substituting the carceral logic of prisons and policing with the similarly institutionalized logic of involuntary mental hospitalizations that may provide temporary stabilization but rarely lead to the lasting peace of mind everyone deserves. And in this way, we are leaving intact the economy that fails to work for anyone born in the last forty years who falls outside of the top 1 percent. If we want to stop being so miserable and start envisioning a better future, we need to adopt a radical imagination.

Dorothy Day was right, in a way that I failed to fully understand in the years I was carting that old, tattered poster around with me: our problems really do stem from our acceptance of this filthy and rotten system. In a certain light, Day's life and work brought me, and thus our journey through this book, full circle back to Kierkegaard and his attacks upon Christendom. It's unlikely Kierkegaard ever intended this quixotic battle to be solitary—one doesn't write about the failures of Christendom without hoping others might also read it and feel similarly moved—but he was by all appearances content to let his convictions rest on the page and within the breadth of his life rather than attempt to rally others to the cause. This may maintain the purity of his work in a way that Day's open communities threatened to collapse (this tension is evident in her diary entries when struggling to define the core convictions of the disparate movement), but this comes at the expense of convincing others to join in the struggle and ensuring that the movement extends beyond the lifetime of any single individual.

Day's condemnation of the entire system should not yield pessimism but rather a new sense of resolve. The current state of affairs in our world does not call for halfway revolutionaries, those who might wish to remake policing without asking the larger questions of how we decided that having a force within society like the police was necessary and why we continue to throw so much of our municipal budgets at them despite limited returns and slashed budgets for other programs that benefit far more people. I become more convinced of the rightness of Day's position as I progress in my social work career.

These issues are not matters of abstract theory to me. For my first internship, which I began just a few weeks after classes commenced, I worked with adults experiencing both homelessness and mental illness. My job was mostly to listen to them and escort them to appointments as necessary, often as part of a team with my supervisors. No amount of reading or study could have illuminated for me how deeply our society hates those without homes, how few resources we provide to help them, and how easily (and cheaply!) the problem could be solved if we provided people with housing. Nearly everyone working in homeless services knows that it would be far cheaper to provide homes and supportive services to those experiencing homelessness rather than ensnare them in a continual cycle of hospitalization, incarceration, and other forms of institutionalization; the data is crystal-clear on this point. Yet lingering myths of deservedness and societal-sanctioned dismissal have meant this policy has virtually no chance of being implemented in the foreseeable future, even if it would cost less in the long run in terms of both human misery and actual dollars.

I found a purpose in doing this sort of work, one that I had lacked in my search for a fulfilling career up to that point. It's not as if my anxiety disappeared overnight. It's still a too-familiar friend, though it's one I have gotten better at managing. I can still feel its presence when stress rises or things don't seem to be working out as I hoped. Doing whatever one can to make a difference, no matter how small, is a great antidote to the hopelessness that too often characterizes our era.

Other things happened while I was in grad school for a second time that helped give me hope. Right after I quit working at the grocery store, I went out for drinks with a coworker. She asked me out of curiosity whether or not I would be open to her setting me up with one of her friends. I couldn't tell whether she had someone in particular in mind or if it was a general question, but I agreed. Her question slipped from my mind as I began my classes and fieldwork, but a few months later, she sent me a text and asked if I was still open to the idea. I was, and she told me to send a Facebook message to a friend of hers. We met up at a dive bar equidistant from our homes and spent three hours talking without noticing the time passing by. Before I graduated, we were married, and years later, we are working on figuring out how to live authentically and wholly in the home we have created, now alongside our two children.

CHAPTER 6

AFTER THE APOCALYPSE

When I first began working on this book, I didn't think so much of my own story would find its way into it. Noticing that a number of my patients had anxieties not easily addressed by the standard etiologies and diagnoses, I was led to reflect upon how philosophy had helped address some of the times I've felt stuck in my own life and thought there might be a book there. As I sat down to write, however, I realized I couldn't offer some coolly worded guide to the fears of the impending apocalypse without writing about how often it has felt like my own world was coming to an end. I didn't settle upon philosophy out of some dispassionate search for meaning; I turned to it because I felt like I was drowning and was desperately searching for a life preserver.

From Kierkegaard, I learned of the risks inherent in existence and the need to take a leap into the unknown with only hope to guide you. This helped give weight and meaning to the time I spent alone in my room during high school, writing bad poetry and feeling desperately misunderstood. Once I settled into college, I felt more secure, able to walk alongside Heidegger and ponder the fact that we find ourselves thrown into a world not of our choosing, with one of the only givens being that we will eventually exit it through death, leaving us to determine how to build a life worth living in the meantime. It would be years before I read Hannah Arendt, but her concept of natality would provide a helpful reframing of Heideggerian concepts in a far more hopeful and generative direction. Aristotle helped me think about how to be good, and that ethics wasn't a desperate plea to avoid eternal damnation but rather the work of a lifetime. And after a switch in academic pursuits, relationships, and careers, Dorothy Day taught me the wisdom of working to bring down the filthy, rotten system in which we find ourselves and to understand that work as an act of love, for everyone who finds themselves broken under its cogs, and particularly for those who find themselves on the outskirts of what the system finds beautiful or desirable.

Books thrive on narrative arcs; lives resist them. There is something within us that wishes our own autobiographies could be so neat. I often hear from patients that they expected to have resolved their problems long ago or that they're surprised to find their anxiety taking different manifestations, even when they thought it was gone for good. In many ways, I have the life I always wanted; I have a wife whom I love, two kids whom I adore, and a career that fulfills me personally and helps make the world just a bit better than it was when I arrived (I hope). Life and experience have given me tools I could not have dreamed of, but I still cope with anxiety on a daily basis and probably will for the rest of my life.

In the introduction, I mentioned a common explanation for anxiety that you may have encountered before—the faulty fire alarm that goes off at inopportune times. I want to suggest a different way of looking at our anxieties, though, particularly the apocalyptic fears about what the future might hold. The purpose of a fire alarm is to get you to pay attention to something, of course, and instead of ignoring it or treating it as a nuisance, we could benefit from listening to it and trying to determine what it might be showing us. It's not very enjoyable to be filled with fear and dread over the climate future of our world, yet we ignore this at our peril. If we are woken up by a fire alarm going off in our house, most of us would not struggle with knowing what to do. From childhood, we are taught that the proper response to such a noise is to leave your surroundings immediately and seek shelter in a safe place. There is no such answer to the apocalyptic anxieties we have considered here, though, no other world to which we can flee. Some try to assuage their fears through making the small gestures they can—recycling and composting and the like. Others numb the fear, either actively through drugs and alcohol or passively through distraction and entertainment. A smaller subset leans into the fear until it morphs into nihilism, a resolve to do what one wants to today and forget about tomorrow. All are understandable; none are satisfying.

Most of us want more than this for ourselves, but admitting that can be a risk. It opens us up to disappointment, the possibility of getting it wrong. I wish I could offer an easy answer to all this, and I wish I had one for myself. My field has often been guilty of offering quick fixes to the foundational issues that ail us mentally. Take this medication and your depression will go away. Meditate twice a day and your anxiety will disappear. Complete this twelve-week treatment for trauma and find the hope and healing you have been waiting for. Life is rarely so easy, of course, even less so when we're confronting possibilities so cataclysmic, so apocalyptic.

Each day, every hour, presents us with a choice, though: We can hope or we can give in to despair. At times, the choice seems obvious; despair is concrete, weighty, while hope can seem light, intangible. We still have the choice, however, and nothing can take that from us. There are times when it seems impossible to choose anything but despair. This is why we need a community around us, a theme that we've seen again and again throughout these pages. Anxiety can make you feel like the lone soldier facing down an invading army. I hope that if you do not yet have that community for yourself, you are able to find it. This work is too hard to be done alone. And we need to take care of ourselves. There is no virtue to be found through ceaseless exposure to human misery. Self-care has become mangled almost beyond recognition in our late-capitalist times, yet at its roots, the concept captures the fact that there will be no one left to do the work if we do not do what is necessary to sustain our own functioning.

In the Episcopal church, the weekly Scripture readings occur in a predetermined three-year cycle called the lectionary. Each week has a set of readings from the Hebrew Bible, the Psalms, the New Testament, and the Gospels that are meant to connect with each other and the particular liturgical season. Some preachers try to connect each reading, others pick one to focus their efforts upon for the sermon. The evangelical churches in which I grew up selected the weekly readings based upon the moods and preferences of the preacher, so over time, I have come to appreciate the steady rhythm the lectionary provides.

Election Day is not marked as a special day in the Episcopal calendar. The lectionary readings are not meant to address its passing, so I didn't know what to expect when I went to church on November 13, 2016. My wife and I went to bed before the results of the presidential election were called, though we had a sinking feeling in our stomachs. I woke up in the middle of the night to find my wife wide awake. "He won," she told me. When I got up in the morning and headed off to work, my coworkers and I cried through our weekly staff meeting, trying to remove evidence of our tears before welcoming our first patients of the day and creating space for them to do the same. I felt in desperate need of hope. It was not lost on me that in other Christian congregations, the election was marked as a victory for "our" side. I had seen the near-universal evangelical acclaim for Trump splashed across my Facebook feed, one of the few ways I stayed connected to people from my hometown, even as I had never felt more disconnected from the area where I was raised.

Mid-November is almost Advent season in the Episcopal calendar, the liturgical season where we await the birth of Christ. In that season and leading up to it, the lectionary readings focus not on the warm glow of the manger but rather the idea that Jesus's incarnation was an apocalyptic event, an unveiling of God and God's love for humankind. So it was with a little bit of surprise that the Gospel reading for that week featured Jesus talking about the end of the world. In the reading from Luke 21, Jesus's followers are marveling at the splendor of the temple in Jerusalem when Jesus prophesies that, one day, the entire edifice would be torn down. Not only that, he says, but wars, famines, plagues, and persecution will happen, but take heart: "Not a hair of your head will perish. By your endurance you will gain your souls."[1]

Such warnings and premonitions are often taken, especially by the evangelicalism which raised me, as elaborate codes to be cracked by the faithful in order to understand what the future might hold. One need not complicate matters so much, however. The Romans didn't keep detailed records of the Jewish peasants they executed for insurrection, but our best guess is that Jesus was crucified around 30 AD. Forty years later, the Romans laid siege to Jerusalem to defeat an uprising in a region long marked by unrest, and once they broke into the city's walls, one of the actions they took was the destruction of the temple. Depending upon your perspective, Jesus's words in Luke are either a prediction of coming events preserved by his followers for later or a reassurance, offered to communities impacted by the devastation, by the Gospel writer, who was almost certainly writing after the destruction of the temple.

The destruction of the second temple was an event that rippled through Israel's history, creating a deep fissure between the before and after times. If we take a plain historical reading of the text, Jesus (or "Jesus") is talking about a particular moment in history that is interesting in an academic way but of little relevance for us today. On the other hand, if we approach the text as I and so many other former evangelicals were taught, it is a prediction of a future yet to come that is helpful as a sort of code for interpreting when things might reach an apocalyptic crescendo in the future. The pastor I heard on that Sunday after the election of Donald Trump, Dan Puchalla, suggested we take a different perspective: Jesus's statements about the end of the world describe a process that we are always already undergoing.

At some point in our lives, we have all lived through the end of our own world, whether that's the death of a loved one, the end of a cherished relationship, or a transition we didn't ask for and hoped we would never have to make. All of us have also lived through the rebirth and renewal of our world through the birth of a child, the promise of meeting someone new, an opportunity opening up where we least expect it. This happens on a national and international level too, of course, whether through the election of a racist demagogue, the changing weather of a warming planet, or the loss of a way of life we thought we were guaranteed. We don't know, cannot know, what lies on the other side of the end of our world. Hope is something we practice, not something we can ever fully grasp.

That helped. It did not end my anxiety about Trump's election, of course, nor did it make me regard subsequent developments with less fear and fury than I might have otherwise. It did reassure me, however, that others have lived through the ends of their world as well. There is an apocryphal saying attributed to Martin Luther: asked what he would do if the world was ending tomorrow, he replied that he would plant a tree. Regardless of what comes next, the good things of life are and will remain good despite all else. The love that we have for one another, for ourselves, and for our world is never in vain. The world is always ending. The world is always being reborn.

NOTES

CHAPTER 1
I examine both of these instances in far greater depth in *(Mis)Diagnosed: How Bias Distorts Our Perception of Mental Health* (Cleveland: Belt Publishing, 2021).

CHAPTER 2
[1] Genesis 22:2, New Revised Standard Version (NRSV).
[2] Genesis 22:3, NRSV.
[3] Søren Kierkegaard, *Fear and Trembling*, trans. Alastair Hannay (New York: Penguin, 2006), 68.
[4] Ibid., 45.
[5] Immanuel Kant, *The Conflict of the Faculties*, trans. Mary J. Gregor (Lincoln: University of Nebraska Press, 1992), 115.
[6] Søren Kierkegaard, *Papers and Journals: A Selection*, trans. Alastair Hannay (New York: Penguin, 1996), 602.
[7] Søren Kierkegaard, *The Sickness Unto Death: A Christian Psychological Exposition for Upbuilding and Awakening*, trans. Howard V. Hong & Edna H. Hong (Princeton, NJ: Princeton University Press, 1980), 5.
[8] Ibid., 5.

CHAPTER 3
[1] Martin Heidegger, *Being and Time*, trans. Joan Stambaugh, rev. Dennis J. Schmidt (Albany: State University of New York Press, 2010), 1, emphasis original.
[2] Ibid., 69.
[3] Ibid., 123, emphasis original.
[4] See Stephen Mulhall, *Routledge Philosophy Guidebook to Heidegger and* Being and Time (London: Routledge, 1996), 121–124.
[5] Simon Critchley, "Being and Time, Part 1: Why Heidegger Matters," *Guardian*, June 8, 2009, https://www.theguardian.com/commentisfree/belief/2009/jun/05/heidegger-philosophy.
[6] *Being and Time*, 180, emphasis original.
[7] Also the title of a classic work by Ernest Becker and a subject of concern for the Freudo-Marxist tradition.
[8] Mark Kaufman, "The Carbon Footprint Sham," *Mashable*, July 13, 2020, https://mashable.com/feature/carbon-footprint-pr-campaign-sham.

[9] Thomas Sheehan, "Heidegger and the Nazis," *New York Review of Books*, June 16, 1988, https://www.nybooks.com/articles/1988/06/16/heidegger-and-the-nazis/?lp_txn_ id=1375541.

[10] Gregory Fried, "The King Is Dead: Heidegger's 'Black Notebooks,'" *Los Angeles Review of Books*, September 13, 2014, https://lareviewofbooks.org/article/king-dead-heideggers-black-notebooks/.

[11] Hans W. Loewald, *The Essential Loewald: Collected Papers and Monographs* (Hagerstown, MD: University Publishing Group, 2000), xlii–xliii.

[12] From her poem "The Summer Day," *New and Selected Poems Volume One* (Boston: Beacon Press, 1992), 94.

[13] Hannah Arendt, *The Human Condition*, 2nd ed. (Chicago: University of Chicago Press, 1998), 1.

[14] Ibid., 5.

[15] Ibid., 9.

[16] Ibid., 9.

CHAPTER 4

[1] Aristotle, *Aristotle's Nicomachean Ethics*, trans. Robert C. Bartlett and Susan D. Collins (Chicago: University of Chicago Press, 2011), 13.

[2] Ibid., 34–35.

[3] Alasdair MacIntyre, *After Virtue: A Study in Moral Theory*, 3rd ed. (Notre Dame, IN: University of Notre Dame Press, 2014), 1.

[4] Ibid., 187.

[5] Iris Murdoch, "The Idea of Perfection," in *Existentialists and Mystics: Writings on Philosophy and Literature* (New York: Penguin, 1999).

CHAPTER 5

[1] Amanda Mull, "The Instant Pot Failed Because It Was a Good Product," *The Atlantic*, June 14, 2023, https://www.theatlantic.com/technology/archive/2023/06/instant-pot-bankrupt-private-equity/674414/.

[2] Josh Bivens and Jori Kandra, "CEO Pay Has Skyrocketed 1,460% Since 1978," *Economic Policy Institute*, October 4, 2022, https://www.epi.org/publication/ceo-pay-in-2021/.

[3] Dorothy Day, *The Long Loneliness* (New York: HarperOne, 1997), 34.

[4] Ibid., 41.

[5] Ibid., 286

[6] Dorothy Day, *The Duty of Delight: The Diaries of Dorothy Day*, ed. Robert Ellsberg (New York: Image Books, 2011), 56–57.

[7] Ibid., 61.

[8] Ibid., 74.

[9] Ibid., 351.

[10] Yoosun Park and Michael Reisch, "To 'Elevate, Humanize, Christianize, Americanize': Social Work, White Supremacy, and the Americanization Movement, 1880–1930," *Social Service Review* 94, 4 (December 2022): 779–835.

[11] Ibid.

[12] "Reporting Child Abuse and Neglect," Illinois Department of Children and Family Services, accessed December 5, 2022, https://www2.illinois.gov/dcfs/safekids/reporting/ Pages/index.aspx.

[13] "Exam Performance Reports for Social Work Schools and Programs," Association of Social Work Boards, accessed December 6, 2022, https://www.aswb.org/exam/contributing-to-the-conversation/exam-performance-reports-for-social-work-schools-and-programs/.

CHAPTER 6

[1] Luke 21:18–19, NRSV.

ACKNOWLEDGMENTS

Many thanks to Anne Trubek for helping shape my thoughts about anxiety and philosophy into a coherent form and to Michael Jauchen and Hattie Fletcher for their careful editing of the manuscript. Thanks also to David Wilson and Phoebe Mogharei at Belt, who helped shepherd this from something existing on my computer screen to a tangible object on the bookstore shelf. I remain thankful for the work Martha Bayne and Dan Crissman put into my previous two books with Belt.

For a book about the importance of community, it is only right that I acknowledge the communities that shape and sustain me still: the Chicago Center for Psychoanalysis, the Claret Center, St. Paul and the Redeemer Episcopal Church, and the University of Chicago Crown Family School of Social Work. Each has contributed to my life in immeasurable ways.

This book has given me an opportunity to reflect upon everything that has led me to the place where I am today. I am reminded of all who have invested in me over the years, including Debbie Fay, Brett Smith, David Fitch, Sam Hamstra, William Borden, Jason McVicker, Stanley McCracken, and Julia Brown. One of the benefits of having spent far too long in school is having a plethora of people who have contributed to my journey.

Thanks to my parents, Cindy Askins and Neil Foiles, my stepparents, Duane Askins and Patty Foiles, and my in-laws, Juan and Suzanne Angulo, who are some of the biggest boosters of my work and who have helped make me the person I am today.

This book would not exist without late-night dorm room conversations and spirited discussions over many years. Thanks to all who have indulged me, especially my perennial interlocutor John Sianghio.

I always assumed I would want to be a parent one day but never knew how deeply I would love it. My daughter Elena and son Edmond make it easy to love. This book owes much to my thoughts about what sort of world they might inherit and how we can make it better for them and their generation. Being their parent is a gift every day.

None of this would exist without my wife, Esther. This book is dedicated to you for your patience with me and all of the support you have offered. All of the stress and anxiety of the past is worth it if it led to our life together. I thought when I was working at the grocery store that my life was over. Little did I know that it was just beginning. I also will always owe Angelina Spear a debt of gratitude for introducing us.

ABOUT THE AUTHOR

JONATHAN FOILES is a psychotherapist in private practice in Chicago. He is a lecturer at the University of Chicago's Crown Family School of Social Work, Policy, and Practice and clinical associate faculty at the Chicago Center for Psychoanalysis. He is the author of *This City Is Killing Me: Community Trauma and Toxic Stress in Urban America* and *(Mis) Diagnosed: How Bias Distorts Our Perception of Mental Health*, both from Belt Publishing.

ALSO BY JONATHAN FOILES

*This City Is Killing Me: Community Trauma
and Toxic Stress in Urban America*

*(Mis)Diagnosed: How Bias Distorts
Our Perception of Mental Health*